DON'T WORRY

GOD HAS YOUR BACK

*Based on life experiences, Light from God's Word
and Supernatural visitations from
our Lord Jesus Christ and His Angels.*

GAIUS A. FORLU

authorHOUSE®

AuthorHouse™
1663 Liberty Drive
Bloomington, IN 47403
www.authorhouse.com
Phone: 833-262-8899

Published by AuthorHouse 04/03/2024

ISBN: 979-8-8230-2296-5 (sc)
ISBN: 979-8-8230-2297-2 (hc)
ISBN: 979-8-8230-2295-8 (e)

Library of Congress Control Number: 2024904194

Print information available on the last page.

This book is printed on acid-free paper.

Apostle Gaius Forlu is an honest, bold, fire brand and God loving preacher of the Gospel with strong inclination and desire to see his generation free from the shackles of darkness unto God's perfect image. This book "Don't Worry, God Has Your Back" is a prophetic insight based on his supernatural experience with the Holy Spirit towards dealing a big blow against the greatest enemy of our faith- worries - and restore us back to a joyful and peaceful life of victory in Christ Jesus.

Everyone must intentionally read this book not only to acquire knowledge and inspiration but also to be forearmed against every stressful situation in life, family, ministry and business.

Please enjoy.

Bishop Dr Emmah Gospel ISONG,

CHRISTIAN CENTRAL CHAPEL INTERNATIONAL,

CALABAR- NIGERIA.

I want to encourage you to take time to not merely read Pastor Gaius's book, but to study it and apply it to your life. Within the pages you will find God given directions as aid you in walking in victory and peace. As you focus upon the Lord great peace will keep your heart and mind (Isaiah 26:3).

Bobby Conner

EaglesView Ministries

In the middle of so many problems and setbacks, so many people are gripped with fear and worry. Apostle Gaius Forlu gives us amazing answers in his new life changing book. He shows us that no matter how big the problem is, God has a greater solution. Apostle paints a beautiful picture of Gods faithfulness, by his personal understanding of God's word, strength, and love. This book is a must read for everyone.

Dr Tim Storey

www.timstorey.com California U.S.A

Don't Worry God Has Your Back is a very timely book for the body of Christ. The stories shared by Apostle Gaius give validity to the special message he carries. When faced with impossibilities he has trusted solely in God and has seen God do miracles. Prayer, fasting, and sacrificial giving are a part of his lifestyle, but he also reveals the key of obedience as being essential to experiencing breakthrough. He is well acquainted with the ministry of the angels, and he knows how to contact God through the power of prayer and praise. Over the years I have ministered in Apostle Gaius' church and have spent time in his home. It is a joy to see his strong marriage and how all his children reverence the Lord. His international ministry is known for signs and wonders. He is a man on a mission and this book will bring strength and comfort for all who read and meditate on its truths.

Apostle Steven Brooks

www.stevenbrooks.org

In his life changing book...” Don't Worry God have Your Back” Apostle Gaius offers you a front row seat into the eternal mysteries of a God who never fails nor abandons the faithful in times of distress. The streams of revelation in the book act as a divine antidote to the cancer of worry that plagues so many people, including many of God's children. It's a story of hope and trust in a God who will not hesitate to deploy His vast resources to protect and prosper His dear children. While acknowledging worry as a common human emotion and sentiment, Apostle Gaius draws on the veins of divine inspiration to challenge demonic protocols and processes that lead people into unhealthy and protracted seasons of worry and stress. Using commonly understood language he wants the reader to know that they don't have to be prisoners of “worry” but realize that God has their back! Don't let Satan steal your moment of breakthrough by suffocating your faith and dreams with worry. I highly recommend this book to those who are desperate for a real and permanent breakthrough.” Don't Worry God have Your Back” is truly an apostolic and prophetic roadmap into a life of uninterrupted peace.

Yours for His Kingdom

Dr. Francis Myles

Bestselling Author: Issuing Divine Restraining Orders from the Courts of Heaven

FrancisMyles.com

Gaius Forlu has written a very timely book. Worry is something that all people deal with at some level. The Forlu's are a family that has received grace of God to overcome fear at every level. The strong, practical insights that Gaius so elegantly writes will empower you to overcome fears, trials, and any other approach of Satan. Do yourself a favor and read this book today!

Dale Everett

Dale Everett Ministries

13138 Courtney Dr.

Frisco, TX 75033

903-372-2032

www.daleeverett.org

In this powerful book, "Don't worry God has your back", you will surely discover the power of the promises of God to deliver you from worry and anxiety.

I know Pastor Forlu and I have seen how his life is a testimony of steadfastness and victory in every ministerial and personal stage.

Pastor Forlu's encounter with Jesus will show how walking in simple but powerful faith will cause the power of God to change you from fearful expectations to glorious moments of victory.

Pastor Tito Caban

Iglesia Avance Internacional. Puerto Rico

I've known Pastor Gaius for about 12 years. In all that time I've witnessed his steadfast commitment to the Lord and His calling. Both he and his wife are an inspiration and blessings to my wife Reshma and myself.

Some years ago, we had the joy of having Gaius and his wife accompany us to Malaysia on a ministry trip. At that time, he was willing just to come and spend time with us and "carry our bags" as he so elegantly put it. I don't believe in letting ministry gifts sit so I encouraged him, and we were able to arrange some small meetings.

As I knew it would, his gift made room for him and opened many doors for him in that nation.

In the same way, this his first book is a grand slam! It is filled with revelation, insights, and sound biblical teaching to help anyone who opens it covers. His testimonies are examples of the goodness of God that is available to all who are called by his name.

I am honored to know Gaius and blessed that he would ask me to write an endorsement for his book! I look forward to many more Gaius!

For His Glory

Dr. Bruce D Allen, www.stillwatersinternationalmissions.com

This book is a powerful tool that the Lord has provided to help you gain the breakthroughs you need be very courageous and strong, and to believe that we are called for a greater purpose, Apostle Gaius, Forlu's straight forward line online style of writing, will challenge you,to study your Bible and build a sound biblical compensation for your faith to stand on,,allowing God to take control of your life. And begin to lean on Jesus.

Dr, Lucy Rael.

DENVER CO.

As we journey through life, though being new creation in Christ Jesus, worrying always present itself as an insurmountable mountain. Many men and women of God who have not dealt with worrying in their lives have fallen short of reaching their potential. We thank God for Rev. Gaius A. Forlu, an anointed servant of the Lord, for writing a book that will help many of us overcome worrying. Writing a book from personal experiences is a game changer. I witnessed transformation in his life and God becoming God in him. His experiences in the book are captivating. I believe before you finish reading this book, the spirit of worry would have left you, your faith in God will become unassailable and you will have a testimony.

Bishop Dr. Israel N. Forlu

www.rolai.tv **MD U.S.A**

I am particularly grateful to God Almighty, for His servant Apostle Gaius Forlu. Before he was born, I knew He is God's own. Growing up, he gave his life to the Lord Jesus at a tender age and has since been planted in the house of the Lord. "Those who are planted in the house of the Lord shall flourish in the courts of our God." (Psalms 92:13 NKJV). God made this scripture come true in his life, even though he passed through difficult situations in life, which God used in revealing Himself, and His purpose and plan for his life. Apostle Gaius grew up as a God-loving and God-fearing son. Always ready to serve the Lord, with such love and passion. He is a man who chooses his words and prefers to say it as in God's word. It was during Gaius' life-challenging circumstances that he discovered that God is the God of impossibilities. I remember after some of his encounters with the Lord, he became God's vessel that always encouraged me and would always say "Mommy don't worry." By the grace of God, the Holy Spirit used his encounters with God, to increase his faith, trust, and total dependency on God, which brought the result of flourishing in the courts of our God. Sometimes when I am about to worry about something, I would remember Apostle Gaius' encounters, and his words "Mommy don't worry, and I will be immediately encouraged to trust God. Thank God for the Holy Spirit. God is faithful. May the Holy Spirit bless all who read his book and free them from the spirit of worry in Jesus name."

Dr Mercy Forlu

Warriors Bride Conference. www.rolai.tv

This is a good book. When you look at today's society, there are so many challenges and obstacles that Christians are facing. Our Christianity and

 faith is being challenged on a daily basis. We really must dig deep within ourselves to apply the word of God and to continually trust in the Lord. Storms of life will always come but as the word of the Lord says, having done all to stand, stand therefor. This book is a reminder that storms will come but there are fundamental principles in the word of God that we can use to make it in life.

We are living in a society that wants solutions from everywhere else but the word of God. As you read this book, you will begin to understand the origin of worry, stress, anxiety and depression, and how to combat these. Also, as a child of God, you have been given authority in the name of Jesus and through the blood of Jesus. By understanding your authority and the principles of this authority, you can make it. The Holy Spirit who is your helper will also guide you on how to access and use this authority.

This book makes a demand of you, to change the way that you approach life. It reminds you to be valiant like Caleb, when you think you are small and insignificant, it will remind you that you are a mighty man of valor, a warrior in Christ. Life's challenges cannot stop you from becoming great, instead God will use those challenges as a vehicle for testimonies to glorify His name.

You will also be reminded that in this journey, God will send you Destiny Helpers. They are very important in crucial and turning points in your life. You must know how to recognize and handle Destiny Helpers, this book will help you do that. This book definitely holds powerful Kingdom truths and Apostle Gaius writes in a way that you will be able to understand the principles in this book so that you can apply them to transform your life, by grace, in ways unimaginable.

I recommend and endorse this book.

Bishop and Prophet, Dr Blessing Samuel Chiza.

Eagle Life Assembly, FIG Ministries

Don't Worry about the Snake bite

A rattlesnake bit one of my sheep in the face about a week ago. Deadliest snake that lives around here. The sheep's face swelled up and hurt her terribly.

But the old rattlesnake didn't know the kind of blood that flows through the sheep. Anti-venom is most often made from sheep's blood. The sheep swelled for about 2 days but the blood of the lamb destroyed the venom of the serpent.

I was worried but the sheep didn't care. She kept on eating, kept on drinking and kept on climbing because she knew she was alright.

Often the serpents of this life will reach out and bite us. They inject their poison into us but they cannot overcome the Blood of the Lamb of God that washes away the sin of the world and the sting of death. Don't worry about the serpent or his bite, just make sure that the Lamb's Blood is flowing through your veins."

Author Unknown

DEDICATION

This book is dedicated to the passionate and devoted saints whom God is raising up in this present age. These individuals are committed to making a significant impact both locally and globally. They are empowered by the Holy Spirit to operate in the supernatural realms of God, demolishing the works of darkness and advancing the Kingdom of God on Earth. Their unwavering dedication and obedience to God's calling are an inspiration to us all. May their lives and ministries bring glory to God and contribute to populating heaven.

ACKNOWLEDGMENTS

First and foremost, I want to express my heartfelt gratitude to God the Father, the Son, and the Holy Spirit. It is through His divine grace and inspiration that my family and I have been blessed with the ability to write this book. I am eternally grateful for His guidance and the endless support He continues to provide us with. Without His presence in our lives, this endeavor would never have come to fruition.

I want to express my deep gratitude and appreciation to my incredible, most beautiful, God fearing, my prophetess and loving wife, Emmanuella Noelle Forlu. Her unwavering love and support have been a constant source of inspiration for me throughout the process of writing this book. Without her selfless sacrifice of time and patience, this achievement would not have been possible.

I am also immensely grateful to my beloved children, Lemuel, Eliana, and Jahzara Forlu. Their unwavering support and prayers have given me the strength and determination to see this project through to completion.

To my amazing parents, Bishop Dr. Israel and Dr. Mercy Forlu, I want to extend my heartfelt thanks. Your unwavering love, sacrifices, and prayers have been a guiding light in my life from the very beginning. Thank you for your continuous support and for being there for me throughout this writing journey.

I would also like to express my gratitude to my dear siblings, Jeremiah Benson, Ryan, Grace, and David Forlu. Each of you played a significant role in helping me along this journey, and I am truly grateful for your love, care, and support.

A special thank you goes to Dr. Francis and Carmela Myles for their invaluable assistance. Your guidance and support have been instrumental in shaping this book. God richly Bless you.

I would also like to acknowledge and thank Mr. Del Arnold and his family for the sacrifices they have made on my behalf during the writing of this book. God Richly Bless you.

Pastor Rudolph and Larissa Foliwe special thanks to your family. God richly bless you.

To all my ministry partners and ministerial friends, I want to extend my sincere thanks for your unwavering support and prayers. Your faithfulness and encouragement have been a tremendous source of strength throughout this journey. We serve a faithful God, and I am grateful for each and every one of you.

Contents

1

❧❧❧

Worry

Have you ever had a sleepless night because of stress and anxiety?

I believe most of us have experienced it at some point in our lives. When we are worried, we don't like doing anything other than thinking about our problems. We lose interest in the activities we generally enjoy. We all desire to live stress-free lives. However, it is impossible because life is another name for trials and tribulations. No one is immune from worry because it is a human emotion. This emotion can be both beneficial and disastrous for us. When we are concerned about our better future, it can bring fruitful results. However, constant stress can cause severe physical and mental health issues.

The Bible talks about worry greatly and helps us understand it much better. In Matthew 6:25–33 (NKJV), Jesus addresses His disciples, saying,

> Therefore I say to you, do not worry about your
> life, what you will eat or what you will drink;
> nor about your body, what you will put on. Is
> not life more than food and the body more than

clothing? Look at the birds of the air, for they neither sow nor reap nor gather into barns; yet your heavenly Father feeds them. Are you not of more value than they? Which of you by worrying can add one cubit to his stature? So why do you worry about clothing? Consider the lilies of the field, how they grow: they neither toil nor spin; and yet I say to you that even Solomon in all his glory was not arrayed like one of these. Now if God so clothes the grass of the field, which today is, and tomorrow is thrown into the oven, will He not much more clothe you, O you of little faith? Therefore, do not worry, saying, "What shall we eat?" or "What shall we drink?" or "What shall we wear?" For after all these things the Gentiles seek. For your heavenly Father knows that you need all these things. But seek first the kingdom of God and His righteousness, and all these things shall be added to you.

Since Jesus spent so many years on earth, He felt every human emotion deeply. He experienced pain, loss, loneliness, betrayal, hunger, and persecution. Despite going through these hardships, He knew full well that worry is a dangerous force that can keep a person from having a genuine relationship with God. He knew that it was meaningless and futile. Trusting in God is all one needs to lead a happy life. In the verse mentioned above, Jesus talks about how God provides food to birds and plants. Unlike humans, these little creatures have no hope for survival unless God stretches out His hand and blesses every living thing.

Similarly, He can also make provisions for us in every circumstance. However, we continue to worry about food, clothes, and other worldly matters because our faith is weak.

We overthink our circumstances. As a result, our minds get cluttered with negative thoughts. Jesus tells us that this is nothing but a lack of faith, and we need to get out of a lifestyle full of anxiety and worry. We need to sit back for a while and glance at the system of nature and see how God controls everything. If He provides for the animals and other living beings, how can He neglect us, whom He values above all creation (see Psalm 8)? Therefore, we need to redirect our focus to the power of God. He is capable of solving our problems and controlling our situations. All we need to do is to trust Him.

We are living in a technological era where everything moves at a rapid pace. Information is streaming faster than ever, and there is enormous pressure on us to be productive in our respective fields. Amid this frenzy, there is a pressing need to maintain relationships, socialize, take care of our health, and pursue our goals all at the same time. While this multitasking can help us stay aligned with the ever-changing world, it can also lead to a stressful and taxing routine that can be detrimental to our mental, physical, and spiritual health in the long run. People often underestimate worry, seeing it as a temporary emotion that helps us become cautious to avoid danger. We believe stress is normal and an indispensable part of our lives.

The truth is that this emotion is the enemy's greatest weapon of choice. Satan tries to distract us by creating circumstances that make us worry or cause internal discomfort in our minds. He makes an effort to push us further away from the Lord's presence. He shifts our minds from positivity by putting so many things on our plates to manage. He makes us fret and overthink our problems. He also creates chaos in our surroundings so that we may not have faith in God. As a result, we fail to believe that everything is under God's control.

Webster defines *worry* as "mental distress or agitation resulting from concern usually for something impending or anticipated." It is essentially a state of anxiety that causes one's mind to dwell on difficulties, troubles, and doubts. It removes faith from the hearts of people.

Long before this became such a huge problem, God made the harmful impact of worry clear through His Word. The Bible is filled with verses where God always advises us not to fear but to trust that He is the Creator and Controller. Through different parables and the stories of prophets and apostles in the Bible, Jesus explained that worry does no good to us. Troubles and hardship are a part of our lives. However, we must practice a life of faith and trust to enjoy God's blessings and favors.

The primary reason why worry continues to rule our lives today is because we try to ignore its existence in our lives. We underestimate its power and try to justify it by coming up with feeble excuses. Identifying the root cause of our problem is imperative to keep our minds from the damaging effects of worry and anxiety. Until you diagnose an illness, you cannot use any medications to cure it. Therefore, you need to know the effects of worry to work toward removing it from your life.

The Five Effects of Worry

We all have experienced the move of God at some point in our lives. We've seen God do something good and unexpected, but when we face a challenging situation, we forget God's goodness. We see impatience and weak faith happening in our present age.

Everyone who has undergone stressful situations in life can feel the effects of worry. These effects can be summarized in five key responses:

1. Fear and discouragement
2. Intimidation
3. Frustration
4. Depression
5. Isolation

The book of 1 Kings describes the five effects of worry in the life of the prophet Elijah.

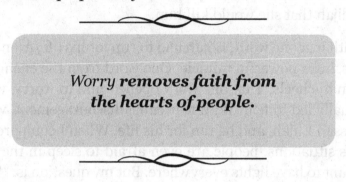

*Worry **removes faith from the hearts of people.***

Fear and Discouragement

The first and foremost effect of worry is fear. As worry takes away our belief and trust in God, we develop a phobia about situations. We may fear failure, rejection, loneliness, the loss of a loved one, illness, or even people in authority. That is because when things are out of our control, and we are weak, we lose hope that the all-powerful God can handle our situations for us. We forget our identity in Christ. When it came to the experience of Elijah, God showed him and the people His true power. He called down fire from heaven, which consumed the sacrifices on the altar right in front of the crowd. The people who witnessed this miracle fell to the ground and worshipped the Lord. Before that, they were exposed to worthless idolatry, which had kept them under bondage for years. God dealt with false prophets by killing all of them. Elijah experienced the real miracle of God that made him know the Lord and move in His power.

Elijah was their man, but all of a sudden, this changed because of one word of adversity. That one word came from Queen Jezebel, who was angry after hearing what happened to the false prophets. According to the Bible, Jezebel represents a wicked spirit—a spirit of control, manipulation, intimidation, and rebellion. Jezebel represents bondage and destruction. She sent a letter to Elijah, saying that she would do the same to Elijah as he did to her prophets. In other words, Jezebel had told Elijah that she would kill him.

With just one word, Elijah had to run for his life, even after witnessing a powerful miracle. One word from the enemy put him on his heels. That one word opened him to worry, which eventually led to fear. With fear came discouragement, which distressed Elijah, and he ran for his life. When I compare it to today's situations, people are even afraid to sleep in the dark and want to have lights everywhere. But my question is, "What are you afraid of?" When you get worried about something, nothing good ever comes from it. It is an entire chain where worry opens to fear, and fear opens up to intimidation.

Intimidation

There may be many things in your life that are terrifying for you. This varies from person to person. However, what is essential is to identify that part of your life that frightens you. Is it your job? A coworker whom you think is doing much better than you? Is it your deteriorating financial condition? Whatever it is, you must realize that this is surfacing because of the underlying worry in your mind. Worry can intimidate and stop us from reaching our highest potential. It stops us from looking at our identity in Christ. Instead, it makes us feel inferior and powerless in comparison to others. I encountered this when I was invited to Nigeria to a large church with about two thousand people in attendance.

There were many great bishops, archbishops, and apostles; and I was the youngest pastor. As I heard them preach one by one, I began to question why I was even there among them. They spoke eloquently, were directed by the Spirit of God, and were polished with experience. On the contrary, I did not find myself capable enough. While I was worrying over the situation, the host told me it would be my turn to minister the following day; this added to my anxiety.

As I returned and walked into the hotel room, I said to God, *What will I say? Everything has been preached.* I just sat there and sighed for the mercy of the Holy Spirit. Instead, the Lord said to me, "Do minister on what you best do that I've laid in your heart. I want you to talk about the glory, and that will cause an activation of the angelic realm more. Talk to them about the angelic realm, about My angels. And let them know that they have to focus on Me, and they will see the realm being activated." I listened to the instructions of the Lord and went to minister the next day.

Generally, the bishops will not attend during the morning service but will show up for the night service. However, when I walked up that morning, some of them were there. I said, "OK, Lord." So I climbed up there, spoke on the glory realm, and encouraged the people to put their eyes on the Lord Jesus. I was given about twenty minutes for the ministration. As I was getting to about the ten-minute mark, the Lord opened my eyes, and I saw fire all over. He told me that the angels of the Lord, carrying His fire, were present and ready to touch everyone listening to me in the congregation. With the leadership of the Holy Spirit, I instructed everybody to stand up, and they stood up, and the power of God invaded. They were falling wherever they were. Things began to happen. The Lord encouraged me that day. One of the bishops said, "You know, I've been trying to teach these things on the supernatural realm around us in my congregation for a long time, but I didn't know how to do it. However, the Lord used you to bring it."

Then, before flying to Africa for this conference, my host told me that my coming and ministry would create an opening for me in the country. He said, "Well, when you come, your gift will make room for you." I stayed there for about two weeks. Bookings took place that same week until I left, and the Lord God did wonders in those meetings.

Being fearful was causing me not to look at what God had laid in my heart. However, when I listened to Him carefully and obeyed Him, I saw His favor over me. I saw what God had placed in me and used it for His glory. Coming to Elijah's example and Jezebel's threat, coercion opens up another spirit that targets each of us. When we open ourselves to intimidation, the other spirit that comes is frustration.

Frustration

Another effect of worry is frustration. Are you frustrated with the level of stress you have in your mind because of your job, life, spouse, or children? It is in every area of your life. The factor that contributes to bringing frustration into our lives is anxiety about our future. We anticipate the problems that may arise tomorrow and end up becoming frustrated. Let's consider the story of Prophet Elijah once again. After defeating the prophets of Baal on Mount Carmel and witnessing the fire of the Lord that engulfed the people, he went through an episode of worry and failure that resulted in frustration as he ran for his life from Queen Jezebel.

First Kings 19:1–2 (NKJV) states, "And Ahab told Jezebel all that Elijah had done, also how he had executed all the prophets with the sword. Then Jezebel sent a messenger to Elijah, saying, 'So let the gods do to me, and more also if I do not make your life as the life of one of them by tomorrow about this time.'"

Elijah was so exasperated that he fled into the wilderness to escape his doom. He said in 1 Kings 19:4 (NKJV), "It is enough! Now, Lord, take my life, for I am no better than my fathers!" Elijah had lost all hope and trust in the Lord. He expressed his desire to die because of frustration. However, the Lord sent His angel, who provided for and protected him in times of trouble. In Elijah's frustration, the grace and mercy of God prevailed.

We need to trust that God is in control. Whether we can see the result before our eyes, He controls everything according to His plan. He will never forsake us.

Depression

Worry causes frustration, which can take us to a place of despair and anguish. If you have experienced depression before, you know it is a dark place where everything fails to comfort you. It is a growing problem in today's society, especially among leaders. Examples from the Bible include Job, who got into depression because of his sufferings; Jonah, who was so downcast that he asked God to kill him; and Elijah, who was so despondent that he prayed for his death as he ran from Jezebel. Similarly, Moses also asked for death when he failed to handle the pressure of leadership.

Depression is an alarming problem that can lead to severe psychological conditions or even death. People suffering from depression may attempt suicide. They may stop practicing self-care and slowly stray away from a happy and content life. This is all a result of worry aggravated over time. People often think that money is the solution to all their problems. However, this is not the case. The world is full of examples of wealthy people, yet they took their own lives because they were depressed and wanted to get away from worldly worries.

Are you at a point where you say "You know, I am tired of living this life" or "Just take me out"? Does depression make you think about committing suicide? If yes, I want to tell you that everything will be fine soon. Taking your life is not the solution. God has given us this life to enjoy His blessings and bounties. He does not want us to wish we no longer want to live. He wants us to rejoice and be happy in all circumstances. Depression is a demonic spirit that needs to be cast out of individuals. We have seen many delivered in meetings and conferences around the world. While there are prescribed medications, we need the blood of Christ to make us truly free.

We had a member who came into the church depressed. He would take antidepressants to treat his bipolar depression. He was on numerous medications. As I was preaching under the leadership of the Holy Spirit, I said, "Depression and bipolar are demonic spirits, and pills can't control spirits. In the name of Jesus, we arrest those demonic spirits, bind them, and cast them to hell!" Immediately, the power of God came to him, and he felt something lifted from him. He was totally delivered and never returned to his medication.

These five effects of worry are all demonic spirits that need to be expelled from people's lives.

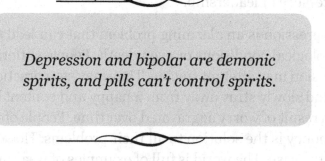

Depression and bipolar are demonic spirits, and pills can't control spirits.

My Melting Point

I encountered some problems when I went to the United States of America. Sometimes, I would go and stay in the basement of a church as a way of escape. I tried to occupy myself in that basement by recording gospel-music videotapes to send to my siblings back in Cameroon, Africa. I read inspiring messages and listened to good music. It was a way of escape for me. Yet I had difficulty sleeping because the thoughts of not being established occupied my mind. I was worried and fretful. Suddenly, the phone line in that basement rang. When I answered the call, a lady was on the other end. She said she was driving and saw the light around 11:00 p.m. I don't remember how she came to know where I was, but she asked me if I had a place to lie down and if I had eaten. I answered no. She took her daughter along with her and drove to where I was in the basement of a church. She gave me the first sleeping bag I had ever had and food. It was, indeed, divine provision.

After that, I spoke to the Lord. I said, "You know what, I'm tired of this. You spoke to me while I was back in Cameroon and said that You're bringing me to the USA to use me and around the world, and You're going to bless me. But look now. Look at where I am. In the basement! In cold winter! You know well that I'm just going through a tough situation."

There were external family issues that were affecting me. After finishing the prayer, I called my dad and said, "So you know what, I'm tired. I'm coming back home." Instead, he encouraged me to continue what I was doing. However, I had already become so frustrated; I was so discouraged that I had already made up my mind. I said to myself, *You know, I'm just going to go out and look for a girlfriend for myself. I'm going to smoke for the first time, I'm going to drink for the first time, and just going to go wild. I don't care anymore. Let whatever happens happen.*

I walked out of that basement and thought of a place to go. I decided to go to a bar that was open till early morning and late in the night on some days. That was the perfect opportunity to go there. I walked down the road and reached the bar. However, to my despair, it was closed. I was flabbergasted; I thought to myself, *Wow, I've never seen this place closed at such a time.* I stood there, put my hands on my waist, and said, "Wow, God, You really mean business with me." I had no option but to leave and return to the church basement.

The following morning, I went to this bar again and asked the man why it was closed. "I came here last night, and I saw that the place was closed."

But the guy contradicted me and said, "No, it was open."

I thought the guy must be lying to me, so I told him again that I had come here. "No, I know it was closed because I came here late last night. It was closed."

He stood his ground and said, "No, it was open then."

I was just so much amazed. In my state of depression, frustration, fear, and intimidation, I had failed to see what was right for me. Yet the grace of God was so sufficient that He made me blind that night because the situation was not favorable for me. He made such a supernatural move to make me think that the place was closed while it was open. That was the grace of God.

You might be at the lowest point in your life. You might be in a place of fear, discouragement, intimidation, frustration, and depression. You might be about to throw in the towel away. Nevertheless, the grace of God is still powerful. The Holy Spirit is speaking to you at this moment. Don't lose all hope; He is right there to help you.

When we are at the worst point, we think we are useless and can't make it in life. That is when God will use His supernatural powers to intervene in your life as He did in mine. When the spirit of depression binds us, we need to be delivered from it. You see, Elijah went through the same situation, which led him to the last stage.

Isolation versus Solitude

In this last stage, the enemy can do anything. There's a difference between isolation and solitude. Isolation is when we pull ourselves away from our commitment. We draw ourselves back from church. We pull ourselves away from prayers. We lose interest in daily activities. We stop studying the Word of God, and we distance ourselves away from the community. Our minds are full of negative thoughts. Such loneliness is a result of depression. Your inner dialogue may sound something like this: *I'm not interested in fellowship. I'm not going to church, work, school, etc. Pastor, I'm not coming to church anymore. I'm not going to pray anymore. They call for Bible studies. No no no no! I don't want to hear anything about God. I want to be left alone. I'm going to isolate myself from everybody—from everything.*

Even the prophets experienced this condition in their lives. Jonah isolated himself, Job detached himself, and even Elijah ran into a cave in a place of isolation. It is dangerous to be in isolation because it makes way for negativity in your life. Isolation makes us perceive everything negatively. We blame everybody for our problems. This state makes it easier for the enemy to fulfill his vision because it is his mission.

John 10:10 (NKJV) says, "The thief does not come except to steal, and to kill, and to destroy. I have come that they may have life, and that they may have it more abundantly."

Solitude is a state where we purposely pull aside to grow closer to the Lord. We believe that no matter how many problems you have in your life and whatever situation you are in, you will continue to push through. *I will be closer to the Lord. I will spend more time on the Word of God, and I'm going to stay committed to my core. I will be more passionate about what the Lord has called me to do for him in this life. I must live a life of purpose.*

Sometimes God has grace and mercy in store for us, as He did for Elijah. Elijah was in the cave in a place of isolation when he heard the voice of the Lord. God asked him this question twice, "Elijah, what are you doing in there?" Similarly, when we isolate ourselves, the Spirit asks us what we are doing in there. He calls us by our names and wants to help us come out of it.

Therefore, we need to remove the mindset of isolation and instead practice solitude if we wish to spend some time alone. Solitude takes us into the presence of God. It takes us to a quiet place where God imparts His divine wisdom, knowledge, and understanding, which are essential to victory over our circumstances. In that place of solitude, we get committed to what God has called us to do. We become determined and focused and then faithfully set out to fulfill His will. Did you notice how worry creates a chain of effects that are worsened if left untreated? It causes fear and discouragement, then intimidation, then frustration, then depression, and then, finally, isolation. It is a step-by-step strategy of the devil to lead us to a place where we can no longer hear the voice of the Lord. Therefore, worry is of utmost concern because we can lose our relationship with the Lord if it dominates our thinking. We can end up in a hopeless situation.

The point is not to discourage you through this. If you find yourself in a state of isolation currently or at any stage discussed so far, I want to tell you that it is still not too late. As long as you are alive, there is hope. You can always cry out to God to take over your situation and lead you out of a life of worry. You can give Him control over your life. Sit back and watch how His grace floods over you. Today, if you are going through this, I encourage you to take the shield of faith and fight against all anxiety and fear. Put on a gospel song and dance and see what happens!

The Lord is asking you what you are doing in your cave. God did not send us into the cave. We are the ones who chose this option. One word from Jezebel, one from your boss, one from your pastor, and one from your brother should not send you into hiding. That is not where you belong. Jezebel's spirit has vexed you. The Bible called Jezebel a spirit of witchcraft. God is with you even when you face challenging situations, even in your weakness, and when you don't feel like the man or woman of God. Remember my testimony? I was at a point where I was going to give up. But the grace of God came and delivered to me.

Also, I would like to share my story about how this message of worry came to me. I moved from Maryland to Indiana, and while I was in Indiana, I had "my wilderness experience." Here, I had an encounter with God that changed my life. One day, I was so worried because I had an excellent job in Maryland and had just received a promotion when the Lord asked me to pack and leave. My wife had just given birth to our child in July, and the Lord commanded me to go in August.

Bishop Dr. Manjoro, my parents' pastor friend from Zimbabwe, was visiting the church. While ministering, this man of God said, "There is somebody here the Lord has been telling you to leave. You must move."

I felt like if I didn't leave, I would die. My wife spoke to me and said, "Honey, I know, but you've got to go."

I had just received a promotion and a nice company car to do rounds at work only. I was getting comfortable. We had planned how we were going to build our home. We had planned on everything, and here, the Lord ordered me to leave. He also instructed us, "As you leave, don't take a secular job."

My brain was spinning with thoughts of worry. My wife had just given birth to our baby. Being a man, I had the responsibility to provide for my family. Nevertheless, I left and went to Indiana. Much to my surprise, when I arrived, I began to see miracles upon miracles. Soon, my wife came and joined me. It surprised me because I was thinking much about my family and our future. "How will we survive the next weeks, the next days?" I questioned every day, but God communicated to me. We have this notion in our minds that the day we see Jesus Christ, we will tell Him all our troubles. We will tell Him everything that is going on and requires answers from Him. Some of us have even written the things that we will tell Him.

Well, let me tell you the truth. When Jesus, the Son of God, walks to you, you don't remember anything. As a result of His glory and holy presence, you fall to your knees. All you experience is love that you don't think of any situation. It is very similar to when you meet the love of your life, but an encounter with Jesus supersedes everything you can think or imagine. Every worry and situation bow in His presence. Such love comes from Him.

One day, I returned from school and was worried about our situation. The following day, I dropped off my wife at a part-time job at TSA. I got home at about past 5:00 a.m. and sat on the bed to pray. While praying, I saw a bright light; Jesus came through it. I could not see His face clearly. He looked at me and pointed His hands toward me, saying, "Son, why do you worry? Have I not said in My word that you should not worry? If I could take care of the birds that fly in the sky and clothe the grass in the field, what more of you? You are valuable in My eyes" (Matthew 6:25–33 NKJV). And He pointed His finger and said, "Listen to this very carefully; each time you worry, you move one step backward from your breakthrough." Did you get that? Each time you worry, you do what? You move one step backward from your breakthrough.

Thus, through this encounter, He reminded me of His promise in the scriptures. He showed me what happens when we worry and why we become worried. I learned that when we pray, the Holy Spirit releases the angel of breakthrough to answer our prayer. The devil sees just a glimpse of your breakthrough coming. Therefore, he tries to bring you into a place of discouragement or worry. The devil knows that when he does put you in such a situation, it will be hard to receive that breakthrough. You don't want worry, bad character, bad behavior, or attitude to hinder our blessings from Jesus Christ. However, when this happens, we have a choice to let the devil take over or hand over the situation to the Lord.

You backed out because conditions were too difficult. Some of you are not hateful, but you put on a hateful face to survive.

17

You allow people to move you out of your personality. You used to be nice, giving, loving, and affectionate. But now, you're no longer any of that. Why? Just because of one word from Jezebel. I know you're living the life of someone beaten as you're in the cave. You are in a place where you eat everything that everyone else eats around you.

This is the world we are living in. Consider this: you stop smiling when somebody acts violently with someone you know. All the happy thoughts disappear, and you start acting as if you do not know that person anymore. Similarly, the enemy is taking your life and backing you further into the cave. And God has sent me to tell you, "Not another day in your cave." He wants to manifest His Glory over your life!

Life had pushed Elijah into a cave. God did not send Elijah into a cave. A cave could be a place of either solitude or isolation.

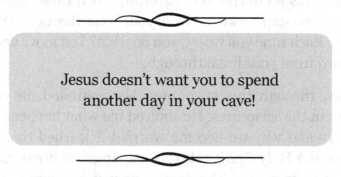

Jesus doesn't want you to spend another day in your cave!

The time has come for you to leave the cave you have been living in because God has called you for a greater purpose. Don't isolate yourself because of the issues of life. Every little thing, such as eating, breathing, and sleeping, is a miracle. Our life needs to be focused on God and His supernatural power to intervene in our lives and in whatever we do. God wants us to live a life free of worry. He wants us to be courageous and strong. Therefore, all that we need to do is allow Him to take control and not let the devil belittle and misguide us.

When your mind is set on the Lord Jesus Christ to receive a miracle, He will always meet you at the point of your need.

Miracle Baby

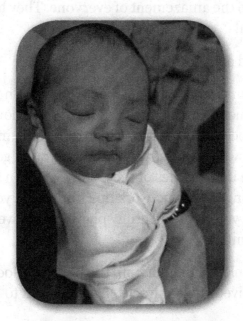

I was ministering at a church called Glad Tidings in Malaysia. I was speaking on the subject of not worrying and sharing my testimonies when the Holy Spirit spoke to me and told me to go into the crowd. As I walked through, the Holy Spirit told me to minister to this couple. They came to this meeting with great expectations for an encounter. The Lord told me to tell her that by this time next year, she's going to have a baby boy. She wept as the power of God came upon her.

When I got back to the USA, I was told she had become pregnant approximately two months after I left. Throughout the time of her pregnancy, the doctors declared she was carrying a baby girl. She kept saying, "The man of God said it was going to be a boy!" The husband, family, and friends continued buying girl clothes. They threw a baby shower on the ninth month,

19

and all the gifts that were brought were all girl clothes and toys, including the decorations. The mother declared and held on to that prophetic word from the Lord spoken to her that she would give birth to a baby boy. When it came time to give birth, it was a boy, to the amazement of everyone. They had to get boy clothes, ha-ha!

When God speaks, it comes to pass.

When your mind is focused on Jesus Christ and His promises, without wavering, your miracle will show up, and you shall experience great results. When you come into the house of God, don't worry about the situation you're going through and don't give in to the lies of the enemy. Trust in the Lord, put on your dancing shoes and worship Him. When you dance and worship Him, you create an atmosphere conducive for the glory of God to manifest.

If this couple did not run into the house of God, they would not have received their miracle. They refused to be in a place of isolation.

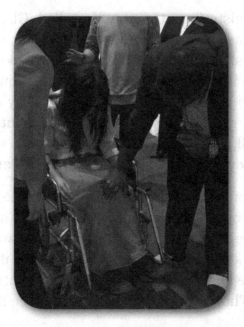

2

❧

My Encounters

Therefore, I say to you, do not worry about your life,
what you will eat or what you will drink; nor about
your body, what you will put on. Is not life more
than food and the body more than clothing?

—Matthew 6:25 (NKJV)

I was born in Cameroon, a country between Western and Central Africa, famous for its ethnically and geographically diverse population. My parents were God-fearing people, who taught us the Word of God from a very early age. Since childhood, they taught me to love and revere God and taught me the importance of attending church regularly. In short, I grew in wisdom, knowledge, power, and spirit.

I gave my life to Jesus Christ when I was eight years old, and at twelve years old, I was given the opportunity by my dad to preach my first sermon to the glory of God. Despite my love and passion for the Lord, I faced every child's challenges. After completing college, my parents asked me to further my studies in Cameroon. The Holy Spirit impressed in my heart that it was time for me to travel to the USA.

They helped me look for scholarships and opportunities to apply for studies abroad. To our dismay, the education programs abroad were too expensive. My father suggested I go to high school back home. He had paid for my fees, but I could not go. I felt strongly it was time to travel to the United States, but I did not know how it would happen. However, when he returned from London, I expressed my concerns again. He contacted the local schools in London, but this wasn't feasible at all. My dad and mom traveled to the United States. Now, as my dad returned from mission work, my mom stayed back in the USA to have several things done. I spoke to her directly about what the Lord had told me. My mom encouraged me to fast for three days to put my desire before God.

She said to ask for God's favor to have my breakthrough. I didn't understand how I could fast for three days consecutively. It seemed nearly impossible. However, my mom was adamant that this was the only way out of the dilemma. Despite the harshness of it all, I listened to my mom; and powered by my faith, I started fasting. Those three days were challenging, but what happened during the fast made me realize the real power of fasting and praying to God.

On the second day of my fasting, I had a powerful dream. I was praying in my parents' room. I was tired and lay on their bed to sleep in the afternoon, and I had a dream; I saw myself driving down a road and saw a platform. I was told to stand on it. I saw millions of people there. Suddenly, I saw a bright big light in the shape of a big star coming down from the sky, and I shouted, "Everybody, look at this light!" However, nobody saw the light except me, so I diverted my focus in that direction. Then, I heard a voice saying to me, "Jump down and go through the crowd."

Suddenly, I ran toward the bright starlight; and instantly, the next thing I saw was a beautiful city. The light was very bright, and it came down on the walls of the building, coming closer to me. I heard a voice say, "Place your hands on the light." I felt awesome, and the power flowed into my body. After I placed my hands on it, it dangled and went upward. After this, my vision ended, and I woke up and spoke to my mom about it. She said the star signified God's favor and was attributed to the Star of David.

Dance with Jesus

On the last day of the fast, I had another dream where I saw Yeshua, Jesus Christ, dancing. He had a beautiful white robe. I could see the scars on His feet and hands, but His face was covered with very bright light. I saw His hair color and style. It was curly dark hair mixed with beautiful gold—I can't really explain it. He was dancing the Jewish way.

As He danced, I also danced with Him. It was an awesome feeling. He had such a beautiful presence that I did not want to leave, but that is all I saw in the dream. When I woke up and told my mom about it, she finally gave me the interpretation of my dreams. She said the first dream I saw showed me the favor of God and the call upon my life to minister to the nations. In the second dream, Yeshua told me that whatever I was going through, I should keep dancing before Him. I should not worry about anything but be joyful in Him.

As I heard her interpretation of my dreams, I looked at the side of the bed and saw my dad's wallet. I knew my dad never traveled without his wallet, but he somehow forgot to take it this time. He had gone to another city in Cameroon to preach. I picked up the wallet beside his bed. Inside the wallet, I found the contact number of the secretary of state, one of the most influential people in the government. I dialed that number, and someone answered from the presidency. The person said, "Who's on the line?"

I replied, "This is the son of Reverend Pius Forlu." He asked me why I was calling and with whom I wished to speak. I said I wanted to talk to the secretary of state. He said there must be a connection for me to have called this line. When the secretary of state got the phone, I told him who I was.

Then he asked, "What do you want?"

With no hesitation, I replied, "I want to go to the United States of America."

He said, "OK, if you want to go to America, you should first get a passport and come within two weeks."

He suggested the solution straightforwardly, but this was not as easy as it seemed. Back then, getting a passport was very difficult. It would require a long time to get it. Besides that, my age would have also been a barrier to acquiring it immediately. However, I took his suggestion to heart; and as soon as I hung up, I called my dad. I told him that we needed to go to the capital city for a visa, and I needed a passport.

He asked me what I had done, and I told him I had called one of the top government departments at the presidency, and he had asked me to get a passport and come to the capital city in two weeks. As I told my dad about the conversation, he became surprised and embarrassed by what I had done. He asked me why I made that call. He was not happy about it at all because of personal reasons. Then he said he would give me the money to get a passport. I took the money and went to the nearby city with my cousin. There, I stood in the long queue of people who had the same purpose as I did. Looking at the long line of people, I knew I would be there for several hours. While waiting in line, I saw a familiar face. I knew I had seen him somewhere on TV. He was a popular secular artist. He had just stormed out of the passport office, obviously furious at the officers inside. He was cursing openly at the officers. The musician's passport renewal was rejected. I thought to myself that if they could reject renewing the passport of a famous person, then I had a few chances of getting it.

Worry wanted to get its way in me, but I recalled my encounter with Jesus Christ. I remembered the Lord instructing me to dance and praise Him despite how hard the circumstances would get. I began to sing and dance on the line. This mere thought shook off the worry and fear. The spirits of discouragement and frustration could not grip me, and I felt strong in faith.

On the other side of the line, a lady from the building came outside and took me from the line into her office. She asked me for my documents. I gave her all I had. She pulled the desk drawer, prepared everything, and handed me the passport in one day! It was quite surprising for my cousin. We called my dad and informed him. He thought it was a joke; my dad was very hard on the phone, saying we should stop pulling his leg and be serious with him. We insisted that we had the passport, and my dad began to thank God on the phone. As we returned, my entire family and cousins living in the same city welcomed me joyfully as if I had won the lottery. Some had been trying to get a passport for years.

They were all waiting to know what had happened that made it possible for me to get a passport within a day. I replied, "It was the Lord's favor." After I received my passport, I went to the capital city the following day with my cousin, Mr. Ayong Bruno. I called the top government official and told him I had the passport. He was also astounded when he heard the news and confirmed whether I was telling the truth.

I had an invitation to the presidency of the Republic of Cameroon the following day. Dr. Daniel Shu, a good family friend, said, "Son, I will give you my best car and driver to take you to the presidency." They were in great surprise at everything happening. Thank god, I was dressed in a suit and my cousin in a shirt and jeans. We all got to the presidency, and I was allowed to go in while my cousin was rejected because he wore jeans.

What a magnificent mansion. I was transported with guards in a beautiful car to the office of this very top government official. My dad also gave me a letter to give to the concerned person there. I handed the letter from my dad to him.

This top government official came out to ask if I knew what my dad wrote in the letter, and I said no. He said that in this letter, my dad said he had nothing to do with all my activities.

He said powerfully, "If we have five people like you who can make such bold moves with full determination, this country will change for the best." While in the office, he called the ambassador to the United States, and they talked. He said his son wanted to travel to the United States of America. The U.S. ambassador said I would be given the visa based on the questions I would be asked at the embassy. Then, my cousin Bruno and I drove to the embassy with the driver assigned by our family friend, Dr. Daniel Shu. I am grateful Dr. Daniel Shu hosted us at his home.

I had five documents: the invitational letter, my passport, my birth certificate, my music certificate, and my ordinary-level certification. I went to the embassy and sat close to a lady in the waiting area. The lady asked for my file. I was very naive. Looking at the file, she laughed and said, "Is this all you have?" I said yes. I asked her if I could see her file, and she gave it to me. I saw all kinds of documents, bank statements, and credit cards in her file. She said her husband is established in the USA. It amazed her that I did not have any heavy supporting papers or qualifications. But I laughed within myself and said, *You don't know where I came from. You don't know who is backing me. You don't know who has gone ahead of me.* I told her how God was directing my footsteps, and I hadn't just come by myself.

I have learned that in this life, you need people who will laugh at you, mock you, belittle you, and look at you as a nobody. The more they do that to you, the more God fights on your behalf.

Remember, He said in His Word that He prepares a table in the presence of your enemies. God won't take you outside and bless you in hiding but inside amid your haters. God loves to manifest His glory in such situations or circumstances.

It was now time for the big interview; everybody who was there for the visa had to go through the interview process. One by one, people went to the visa window and came out disappointed. Before me, the woman's turn for the interview came. To my astonishment, they rejected giving her the visa. Next was my turn, and I stood in front of the interviewer, who asked me one major question, as seen below. I smiled and thought of how God was with me through it all. In my mind, I repeatedly told myself I would not worry at all.

The interviewer asked me, "Are you a musician?"

I said, "Yes."

He said, "How did you become a musician?"

I told him about myself. I told him that I played various instruments at church. He asked if I could sing, and I told him I could. Then, he asked me to sing, and I followed his request. "You don't have to worry, and don't you be afraid."

I began singing, "Joy comes in the morning, troubles they don't always last, for there's a friend in Jesus, who will wipe your tears away and if your heart is broken ..."

He stopped me there and asked, "Who wrote the song?"

I said, "Kirk Franklin."

Next, he said, "Can you sing like an American because you need to sing like an American if you're going to America."

I told him I could try. I had a solid accent, so I was sure that singing in an American accent would not be easy. Despite this drawback, I tried it. As I began to sing, the people in the entire place began to clap for me. The presence and glory of God came into the area I was in the embassy, and it was visible in the way the interviewer's eyes became watery and his face turned red. The interviewer became touched by the song. Others working at the back of the interview were clapping, including the lady who was waiting to see what would happen to me. The interviewer was greatly touched and said, "Thank you so much. Your song touched me and others." The interviewer looked at me and said, "You know what, come back at 4:00 p.m. and pick up your visa."

I was amazed at what had just happened. As I walked out, the lady looked at me and hugged me. She admitted that God was really with me. However, I had a problem. When I came out of the embassy, I didn't even have the money to pay for the visa pickup! I called a number that my dad gave me in case of an emergency. It was Bishop Chris Raymond. He came and gave me the money. However, when I told him about the news of getting a visa, he was also surprised. My family, especially my dad, asked me again and again. When my cousin insisted I had it, my dad cried on the phone, praying and thanking God for such favor. My mom also had tears of joy and was dancing on the phone. They were astounded by how quickly I got it. Upon picking up my passport, I was informed that only another guy and I had a visa to the USA. My family and cousins rejoiced with me. And then, I began my preparations for the journey. Your praise to God will always create a path for you.

> When God favors you, people will think your story was made up. Your praise to God will always create a path for you.

I flew and landed in the United States. When I got to the immigration office, the woman looked at my documents and saw my invitation letter. She called me to the side and told me that I had arrived on the day the invitation had already expired. I told her that she was wrong. The date of my invitation letter was exactly the twenty-fourth and twenty-sixth of April, and if I am not mistaken, I had landed on the twenty-sixth. She asked me why I was there when the program was over, and I said, "Ma'am, if you look at the invitation, it says 24 and 26, which means it could continue from the twenty-sixth onward."

Then she asked me who had given the invitation, and I said my cousin, who lived then in the State of New Hampshire. They kept trying to call my cousin for hours, but the lines didn't go through. The officer took me to another office. We went all the way to the chief of immigration at the airport, who asked the same questions and later told the lady officer to decide on my case. I came across people getting ready to be deported back to their various countries or being processed for jail for one reason or another. The office told me to take a look at them. I told the lady officer the same thing. This lady brought me back to the table and said, "You know what, Gaius, you should not lie to us when you come back next time."

I said, "I'm not telling a lie to you. That is the truth, as my invitation letter says it."

The lady officer said, "Well, I will let you go through." She escorted me with other officers to my luggage. I was the only passenger left. The floor was empty, and it was late.

When I came outside, I saw that everybody waiting for their families had already left. I came out and saw just my mum, aunt, and cousins waiting for me. My mom, aunt, and cousins were outside, praying for me. After a long wait, they knew something was wrong. I was gladly welcomed when I came out, and we called my cousin in New Hampshire. He had forgotten that the program for which he had sent me an invitation had been canceled. He didn't even know that I was arriving in the USA on that day. He was busy on the phone while the immigration tried to call him repeatedly. He unplucked the phone line to use for the internet, so he could not be reached. Thus, this was the favor of God that had led me from Africa to the United States. By God's grace, I am now a United States citizen. I experienced the favor and glory of God in manifestation over my life. There, at the airport, I was praising and worshipping the Lord within me. I always remembered the encounter I had dancing with Jesus Christ.

Since childhood, I have been taught about the Word of God and was always given teachings from the Bible. Nevertheless, I was sometimes weak in faith regarding worrying and anxiety. It may have shown up more clearly over the years, but it has always been a part of me since I was a kid. I will look at my parents and ask how I would manage a home as they do. I knew someday I would leave home. I had always been fearful, especially when the most significant time of my life came when I had to decide on my university. As every rejection came and all doors seemed to close, my heart sank because of discouragement. I was too young, and these things were a matter of concern for me. However, my mother advised me to deal with the impossible things with the help of fasting and prayer, and that's when I had this remarkable encounter with the Lord Jesus dancing with me.

Webster defines *worry* as "mental distress or agitation resulting from concern usually for something impending or anticipated.' Other words that can describe it are *anxiety* and *fear*. While this is a universal human emotion that can help us deal with many problems and make us reflect on situations, it is also an enemy that can adversely affect us. Worry breeds in the mind, but in the long run, it shows physical signs and symptoms of its existence. There are many physical diseases and psychological disorders that result from constant worrying.

Worrying can spread its impact quickly. As a person worries, their vision of faith may become clouded, and their perception may turn negative. Worry is the opposite of faith, so we must choose between the two. Jesus recognized the devastating impacts of worry as He experienced every human emotion closely. He could relate to whatever we feel, and therefore, He warned against the adversary that anxiety is.

He said, "Therefore do not worry, saying, 'What shall we eat?' or 'What shall we drink?' or 'What shall we wear?' For after all these things the Gentiles seek. For your heavenly Father knows that you need all these things. But seek first the kingdom of God and His righteousness, and all these things shall be added to you. Therefore do not worry about tomorrow, for tomorrow will worry about its things. Sufficient for the day is its trouble" (Matthew 6:31–34 NKJV).

The Heavenly Father is there to care for all our needs, and He can provide for us without asking Him. Therefore, we must not allow anxiety and worry to rule our hearts and minds. I have seen His promises come true. I have seen the Lord taking over my circumstances and preparing a way for me.

All I had to do was dance and praise God. Dancing expresses joy, and the Lord asked me to do that. And He is asking you to do the same. As I rejoiced in faith and rebuked the spirit of fear and anxiety every time it tried to take control over me, I found that God walked before me the exact way He did with the Israelites in their journey out of the land of slavery. I was also preparing for a trip ahead, and as I let go of worry, He took care of all my tomorrows.

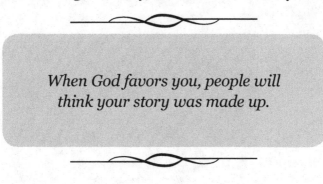

*When God favors you, people will
think your story was made up.*

3

❧❦❧

You Are a Supernatural Being

When God created man, He made him after His likeness and breathed into his nostrils, giving life to his lifeless clay body. He gave him His attributes of purity, holiness, and immortality, fashioning him with absolute compassion and joy. He then took a rib out from his side and created a partner just like him to be his companion, whom He called a woman. Finally, God placed the two in the Garden of Eden in His glorious presence. He would communicate with them directly, and they would freely enjoy His fellowship.

God did not want to create a man to flaunt His creativity but to have someone with whom He could have close companionship. He wanted someone with whom to share His love, joy, and authority. That is why when He created Adam. He gave him sovereignty over every other created thing: the birds, the beasts of the field, and the sea creatures. He gave the honor to Adam to name all the animals. Moreover, God gave them the liberty to eat every fruit in the garden, giving all the plants and trees in his care.

Genesis 1:26 (NKJV) clearly expresses God's sheer delight in handing authority to man: "Then God said, 'Let Us make man in Our image, according to Our likeness; let them have dominion over the fish of the sea, over the birds of the air, and the cattle, over all the earth and over every creeping thing that creeps on the earth.'"

Thus, God gave Adam and Eve the privilege to call what He created their own. He granted them the honor to be in His presence despite being the God of the whole universe. The man, created out of the dust of the earth, was elevated to such a high place where no other creature deserved to be. Following that, He gave them His final command, which was the chief purpose behind their creation, "Then God blessed them, and said to them, 'Be fruitful and multiply; fill the earth and subdue it; have dominion over the fish of the sea, over the birds of the air, and over every living thing that moves on the earth'" (Genesis 1:28 NKJV).

That was the initial state of creation where man bore the image of God and was sent out to spread it across the face of the earth. In all this, God was alongside them, watching over them and communicating with them, so the world was in complete harmony and peace. However, this oneness was short-lived, as the enemy distorted God's image by enticing man to disobey God. As sin entered, death entered too; and along with it, a gap widened between God and man. The Bible tells us in 2 Corinthians 6:14 that light has no fellowship with darkness. Therefore, as the darkness of sin engulfed man, God banished them from His presence and took away all honor from them.

As you can see, before sin came, man was in the presence of the Lord. Here, there was absolute serenity, purity, and joy engulfing in His glory. There was no race of frustration, depression, fear, or worry. In this atmosphere of God's glory, Adam and Eve were capable of flourishing and had control over the things around them. If Adam had been worried, he would not have dealt with ideas with a calm and collected mindset. He would have been anxious thinking about the load of responsibility that God had handed him. However, Adam knew that the God of the universe had given him the task of ruling over creation. Therefore, he was going to bring it to completion through them.

Originally, Adam and Eve had been given physical bodies comprised of a spirit. This spiritually awake state enabled them to understand and communicate with God in the physical realm. On the contrary, when sin came, Adam and Eve died spiritually. Therefore, they also lost that connection with God in the physical realm. To put it in simpler words, to have a relationship with God where He would manifest Himself physically, one must be connected to Him spiritually. With spiritual detachment, one would naturally be banished from the presence of the Lord.

Consider how Adam and Eve died spiritually and lost their immortality. When they detached from God in terms of attributes of purity and holiness, they also disconnected from Him physically. Everything that took place on a spiritual level was manifested physically. Therefore, it is crucial to understand that God intended to make us spiritual beings with physical bodies since the beginning. In essence, we were supernatural beings, reflecting the person of God in this manner as well. The Bible breaks down the person of God in the following way: the Father, the Son, and the Spirit. The sovereign God of all creation had a spirit and a body. Even though Jesus manifested Himself in the most humanlike attributes and presented His characteristics on a physical level, He is essentially Spirit.

The Gospel of John 4:24 (NKJV) states, "God is Spirit, and those who worship Him must worship in spirit and truth."

Therefore, when God created man after His image, He also gave them a spirit to reside in their physical bodies. But when sin came, the spirit of man died.

However, God's unrelenting compassion did not end. He gave us yet another chance through Jesus Christ to gain restoration in all aspects. Not only did He want them to be revived spiritually, but He also wanted to bridge the gap between men and Himself. Moreover, He allowed men to mend their relationship with God by repenting from their sins and believing in Christ. By this, the Spirit of God would come and dwell in their mortal bodies once again. It would restore that purity and holiness and return that authority and control they previously had. Therefore, now, through Jesus Christ, we have been revived spiritually. However, our carnal nature often interferes with our lives and overpowers us in the form of fear and worry.

That is why we need to recognize and acknowledge that we are supernatural beings. Our focus must be on the spiritual bounties, not on the physical ones. Our lives outside are directed by what is going on inside. Therefore, we must not be driven by fear and worry because that will harm our situations.

We must see the Holy Spirit working in His fullness in our lives. Living in this world where temptations and all kinds of distractions surround us, it is challenging to be upright all the time. However, we can always redirect our focus to our inner selves, where the Spirit of God is alive and actively working. We need to acknowledge His presence repeatedly. As we do, we will slowly give less power to the carnal and more to the supernatural. We can do this by stopping worrying and reaching what God has deposited within us. We need to leave that carnal side of us and let the supernatural come out. That is when we will regain that state where Adam was—close to

God, in complete peace and faith, with endless possibilities to flourish.

Today, a significant part of the church's focus is on living in the natural. Church leaders focus on tithing, increasing the number of people in the congregation, and so forth. However, very few are focused on working on the supernatural realm in the believers' lives and releasing the glory of God. God wants us to quit worrying about the number of people or the finances and instead keep the faith He has given to us. He wants us to be spiritually faithful, and only then will we be able to flourish in the outer realm of His glory.

Our present is now, but it is outside of us, while our future is now and inside us. Our entire future already belongs to us in the spirit realm, but worry can hinder us from having it.

Worry in our carnal minds can cripple us mentally, emotionally, physically, and even spiritually. While the spiritual side is primarily underestimated, we must understand that it can determine all the other aspects of our lives. We need to focus our minds on positive things to activate our Spirit and take complete control of the physical side.

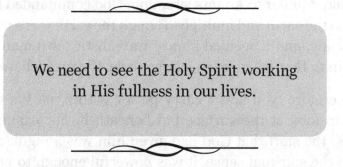

We need to see the Holy Spirit working
in His fullness in our lives.

We may be busy looking for things outside and being anxious, creating scenarios in our minds. However, if we set aside worry, we can steer our future by aligning it with the call of God. We can give birth to our destiny and bring the purpose God has placed within to reality.

The prophets of the old lived in an era where the people were detached from the presence of God. However, they knew how to tap into the spiritual side of men and birth it out into the natural realm. For example, Ezekiel spoke to the dry bones to live again, as commanded by the Lord,

> What seemed ordinary to men was of exceptional use in the eyes of God.

> Again He said to me, "Prophesy to these bones, and say to them, 'O dry bones, hear the word of the Lord!' Thus says the Lord God to these bones: 'Surely I will cause breath to enter into you, and you shall live. I will put sinew son upon you, cover you with skin, and put breath in you, and you shall live. Then you shall know that I am the Lord.'" (Ezekiel 37:4–5 NKJV)

That was what the Lord showed him spiritually. God had to cause him to see what was available for him in the spiritual realm. Even though he had not seen it beforehand, he proclaimed it out loud. Similar to Adam's situation, God commanded him to subdue the earth and multiply. Though the earth was a massive landscape, and it seemed almost unrealistic for a man and a woman to flourish on such a large scale, the two believed.

Therefore, you and I carry power within us. We do not need to look at the surface but beneath it. For example, to Moses, the staff that God had given him was a regular stick; but in the spiritual sense, it was powerful enough to produce water from a stone and to part the Red Sea. Another example of what difference there is in the eyes of a carnal being and a supernatural being is the incident in 1 Kings 18:41–19:8

(NKJV). While the servant saw a cloud, Elijah saw the rain before it could even happen.

Similarly, we must lift our focus from the present situation, look deep within, and tap into our future. We need to know who we are. We need to speak positively to ourselves as well as our circumstances. When we talk about living from the outside in, we mean allowing the situations to dictate how we should react. That fills our surroundings with fear and worries, as the enemy always creates hopeless circumstances around us.

In comparison, living from the inside out can miraculously affect our surroundings. As we understand that Christ Jesus is within us and we are the dwelling place of the Spirit of God, we will think positively in alignment with the will of God. We will not let external situations direct our emotions. We will allow the supernatural to manifest in the natural.

> As Christians and believers of Christ, we are taught to live from the inside out, not the outside in.

Jesus says in John 7:38 (NKJV), "He who believes in Me, as the Scripture has said, out of his heart will flow rivers of living water."

These living waters are the spiritual realities of Christ that can be manifested outside. Within us, we hold power over our circumstances and our future. That can only be achieved if we believe in Christ and let His Spirit control us from within. We need to let the living waters flow freely. That dam will hinder us from exercising the authority that Christ has given to us. It will impede the Spirit and the glory of God from moving in our lives and working freely.

However, if we can surrender to God our fears and worries, believe in what God has placed inside of us, and put our faith and trust in God, we can break all spiritual hindering dams and bondages and unleash the power within us. We can break free from the slavery of fear and oppression and allow God's Holy Spirit and glory to manifest His spiritual blessings outside of us. So now, when we approach those difficulties that the enemy is causing in our surroundings, we must approach them by the Spirit of God within us and a shout of praise. We are supernatural beings, and we can affect the situation. We can control and transform the surrounding situations with the power of God residing in us.

> If we are in a state of fear and worry, we will build a dam around the water inside us.

First John 4:4 (NKJV) says, "You are of God, little children, and have overcome them because He who is in you is greater than he who is in the world."

That is why we also have already overcome our difficulties because of the Spirit in us. We only need to allow Him to work by putting aside our worries and doubts.

When Jesus came to the earth, He had the same human attributes. He had the same emotions, weaknesses, and fleshly nature waging war against His spirit within. However, throughout His days on earth, He diligently fought against it and allowed His spirit to rule over His nature. He walked and lived from the inside out, which is why, despite being surrounded by sinful people and the devil's temptations, He did not fall prey to them. Instead, He walked in prayer and made sure to reflect the perfect image of the Father through Himself, the task that the first human beings failed to accomplish.

Adam and Eve were created after the image of God, but they failed to retain it. However, as Jesus came in the fullness of God and men, He chose to walk by the Spirit to keep that image intact. He knew that the world was more prone to the devil's temptations than those of the Garden of Eden. The garden had the presence of God in it, yet the enemy crept in and misguided the man and woman. The world became a place deprived of the presence of God. There was wickedness and sin everywhere. He was to be extravigilant to deal with the temptations, focusing on His inner self and not on the carnal urges.

As Jesus practiced this lifestyle, it was manifested in the situations around Him. His connection to His supernatural realm enabled Him to perform miracles and marvelous works that no one could comprehend. Where an ordinary person saw the physically disabled and blind people, Jesus saw how they could be healed. Therefore, they were liberated from their sufferings when He placed His hand on them.

Today, we can live a life like Jesus. Even though Jesus is God, He shares His authority with His believers. It is similar to how God shared His authority with the first humans. Jesus Himself talked about this in John 14:12–14 (NKJV), "Most assuredly, I say to you, he who believes in Me, the works that I do he will do also; and greater works than these he will do, because I go to My Father. And whatever you ask in My name, that I will do, that the Father may be glorified in the Son. If you ask anything in My name, I will do it."

With the spirit of Jesus, we can perform the same wonders He performed and overcome the trials and tribulations this life offers. In Him, we can defeat the enemy and our fleshly desires. In Him, we can live fruitful lives filled with endless possibilities. Jesus has done it all for our sake and has drawn a roadmap for us to follow so we can live like Him.

Hebrews 4:15–16 (NKJV) states, "For we do not have a High Priest who cannot sympathize with our weaknesses, but was in all points tempted as we are, yet without sin. Let us, therefore, come boldly to the throne of grace that we may obtain mercy and find grace to help in time of need."

We have a High Priest who overcame everything for us so that we may get that lost image of God back through Him. He sacrificed His own life to bridge the gap between the Father and us. Therefore, we need to believe in Him and give His spirit all control over our lives. Just like Him, we need to live inside out. We need to stay connected to our spiritual man so that the carnal side loses its power over us. We need to acknowledge that we are supernatural beings, and all that we decide and believe on the inside will take shape on the outside. As supernatural beings, we carry the power to overcome anything that comes our way. Therefore, worry, our physical state of mind, must no longer direct our perspective and outlook on life. Instead, we should only hold on to what the Holy Spirit has placed in our hearts; by this, we will experience the glory of God over our lives.

4

<hr />

Supernatural Provision in the Glory

So do not worry, saying, "What shall we eat?" or
"What shall we drink?" or "What shall we wear?"
For the pagans run after all these things, and your
heavenly Father knows that you need them.

—Matthew 6:31–32 (NKJV)

As the devil continues to govern the world and lays various traps to encompass us with trials and temptations, it seems almost unimaginable not to have to battle against the feeling of worry. Every day, there is a new thing to fret over. While someone may worry about making ends meet, someone else may be worried about their job, school, or career. Even if you successfully overcome the stress caused by these reasons, there may be other situations in your daily life where you cannot help but surrender to the troubling thoughts.

Traffic jams are one such situation that everyone can relate to. While traffic cannot cause significant damage, it can still seem like a mountainous barrier, especially when you are already running late for an important meeting or event. Something as simple as that can give you bouts of anxiety. Therefore, it would not be wrong to say that worry is a common and consistent enemy we all have to fight. However, it still doesn't mean we should allow it to lord over us.

We can keep replaying our anxious thoughts in our minds. Still, they will not make any difference to the circumstances we are going through. Therefore, worrying is vain and useless because it does not benefit us in any way. Remember, you move one step backward from your breakthrough each time you worry.

While in Indiana, I returned from school, and my wife showed me the electric bill. It was a disconnection notice for the following day. Guess what we did? We remembered an encounter I had with Jesus Christ. Jesus taught me personally a powerful key to use amid trials. Back in Cameroon, God told me He would bring me to the USA. I did not know how that would happen. My mom instructed me to take a three-day fast. On the last day of the fast, I was praying in my parents' room, and I suddenly slept off on their bed.

I had a dream, and in this dream, the entire atmosphere was so beautiful. The sky was blue with beautiful, bright lights. Then, in front of me came this handsome man. I could see the scars on His feet and hands. His hair was a mix of gold and dark colors. I can't really do justice to the color blend. His face was so bright, and I could not see through. His garment was glittering and very bright. He began to dance in the Jewish style. Immediately, I began to dance with Him. As He moved forward, I followed behind Him, dancing. Then He said dancing, praising, and worshipping Him should be a lifestyle and that I should dance amid trials or difficulties. This was an awesome encounter with no other person than our Lord Jesus Christ.

Based on that encounter, my wife gathered the bills and brought them to the center of the living room. As they were placed at the center, she went to the computer, looking for the hottest African gospel. She found one good song; we gathered at the center of the living room, climbed on the bills, and danced on them. While dancing and praising God on the bills, the doorbell rang. I rushed down the stairs to the door while my wife was still dancing. I opened the door, and to my surprise, it was our pastor! I don't know how he knew our address. He said, "Hello, my man, how are you?"

I said, "Doing well."

The pastor explained that while he was driving, the Holy Spirit spoke to him to make a U-turn and drop off a check to us. Glory to Jesus! When I got the check, it was the exact amount to quickly cash before the banks closed to make the payments available.

My beloved, God will always make a way when we put Him first. When you go through a season of trials or lack again, praise and dance for Him.

Remember Jehoshaphat in 2 Chronicles 20 (NKJV)? The Bible says three nations gathered to battle against Jehoshaphat. We see that the very first thing that approached King Jehoshaphat was *fear*, but he did not yield to it. It's effortless to yield to the spirit of fear in the middle of trials. I came across a word that says, "Be not afraid because

- fear can rob you of God's promise for your life;
- fear can convince you that you will never see the goodness of God; and
- fear can destroy your motivation, faith, ability, confidence, and purpose."

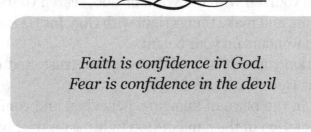

I believe Jehoshaphat understood that failure lies in the place of fear or worry. Immediately, King Jehoshaphat resisted the spirit of fear and worry and decided to seek after God. Breakthroughs occur when God is put first. The king sought the Lord in prayer and fasting with the entire nation. They reminded God of His promises, and the Bible says in verse 14 that "the Spirit of God came upon Jahaziel." Jahaziel means "whom God watches over." The Holy Spirit spoke through him to the nation that they should not be afraid or dismayed of the great multitude, for the battle is not theirs but God's. The children of Israel won't need to fight the battle. God instructed them, "Position yourselves, stand still, and see the salvation of the Lord who is with you."

First, God said, "Position yourselves." Whenever you want to see the manifesting power of God's glory upon your life or family, you must position yourself for the breakthrough. Do you want supernatural provisions in your life, family, ministry, or nation? Position yourself. It wasn't necessary for them to devise a battle strategy or fear defeat. They had to follow instructions.

What does it mean to position yourself? It means to be in the right standing with God. Remember Joshua 3:5 (NKJV): "And Joshua said to the people, 'Sanctify yourselves, for tomorrow the Lord will do wonders among you.'"

How do you do this?

- Align yourself with the Word of God, search yourself of any sin, and make things right with God, for He is about to do wonders on your behalf.
- Position yourself in confidence, faith, trust, and belief in the God who fights for you.
- Stay in the place of knowing, believing, and confident expectation of the hand of God fighting on your behalf.

God also told Jehoshaphat and the nation of Israel to "stand still."

What does it mean to *stand still*? God was telling them to wait or rest. In the place of rest, strength is renewed. Isaiah 40:31 (NKJV) said, "But those who wait on the Lord shall renew their strength; They shall mount up with wings like eagles, They shall run and not be weary, They shall walk and not faint."

By God's grace, most of the encounters I have had with the Lord through the word of knowledge and what to speak before services all came from the place of rest. Your mind must be in the place of rest to make wise decisions, especially to experience the supernatural move of God over your life and family. From the place of rest in body, soul, and spirit, you can see and experience the power of God's manifestation, as seen numerous times in the scriptures.

> Don't be afraid to cry out to God. A hopeless person can't dream or know a miracle. You can pray and miss, but you can never praise God and miss.

We win battles from the place of rest with no worries. As we mentioned earlier, before the multiplication of bread and fish in Mark 6:39, Jesus commanded them to sit down. Until they were obedient to sit, they were not in a position to receive the miracle.

48

From the place of rest, God gave Jehoshaphat a divine strategy for battle, and the strategy was to sing and praise God! It's difficult to rejoice amid worries or chaos. The devil desires to see you walk around twisting your face, murmuring, grumbling, and complaining. The devil and his demons know that if they can keep us in that state, nothing tangible comes from God. It takes men and women of faith to dance and praise God amid trouble. God desires that we praise Him when going through hell on earth. When we do, God Himself comes down and fights on our behalf. If He did it in the Bible days, He is still doing it today.

> Constant meditation on the Word of God puts us in a place of rest where heaven is opened for a raw manifestation of God's power for the world to see.

Carrie ten Boom said, "Faith sees the invisible, believes the incredible, and receives the impossible. Faith is to accept the impossible, do without the indispensable, and bear the intolerable."

The Bible says in 2 Chronicles 20:22 that as they sang and praised God, the Lord ambushed the enemies of Jehoshaphat, and they killed themselves. When the children of God arrived, all they saw were dead bodies. And guess what? The children of God saw and gathered an abundance of valuables that took three days to gather. It's been said that from the time Jesus walked on this earth until now is early three thousand years. Jesus died on the cross and was resurrected on the *third* day. It was on the *third* day Abraham saw where God was taking him.

Prophetically speaking, we are in the season of gathering. Whatever God placed in you that has been dormant is resurrecting now because the same Spirit that raised Jesus Christ on the third day is the same Spirit that resides in you.

49

That same Holy Spirit provides for a supernatural move of deliverance and supernatural provision. You shall see what God sees about you! I speak clarity into your mind and eyes in Jesus Christ's name. God is giving you rest in this season.

Being anxious and running after material things is a pattern that the entire world follows. The fast-paced technological world has made people accustomed to living a life where they are in control. Therefore, when circumstances arise where they can do nothing but watch helplessly, they lose patience and begin to worry. Jesus shows us that, being children of God, we must not strive to control things but rather place everything in His hands. We must seek His Kingdom and believe He will provide for us just like He provides for the birds of the air.

> Your total dependency on the Holy Spirit will create a constant open heaven over you.

Living and spending most of their time with Jesus, the disciples recognized the value of God's kingdom over any worldly things. They had learned to be content in the Lord's fellowship, which motivated them to leave their homes, belongings, and professions to accompany Jesus in His ministry. As they went through each day, they witnessed how God made provisions for them wherever they went, and this lifestyle increased their faith daily.

Paul talked about this increased faith in 2 Corinthians 5:6–7 (NKJV), "So we are always confident, knowing that while we are at home in the body we are absent from the Lord. For we walk by faith, not by sight."

Paul and the other disciples recognized that they were supernatural beings. They were not merely flesh and bones living ordinary lives. Rather, the Spirit of God was at work within them. Therefore, they set their eyes on the unseen and patiently waited for God's supernatural provision. As they did this, God Himself provided for them supernaturally. Whether they were surrounded by difficulties, persecution, sickness, or poverty, God came to rescue them when they called out.

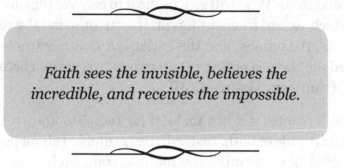

Faith sees the invisible, believes the incredible, and receives the impossible.

The Word of God contains many stories where God extended His arm to bless His people supernaturally. The story of the Israelites' escape from Egypt is one prominent example in the Old Testament. As the Israelites set out from Egypt, they had a long journey to complete before reaching their destination in Canaan. On this journey, they would experience many challenges, such as the harsh weather and the unavailability of food, water, and clothing. The Israelites who had set out were in large numbers. The route was only an eleven-day journey by foot, but because of their disobedience and rebellion, the eleven days turned into forty years. Even if they had carried food and water, it would have still been consumed along the way, leaving them starving.

As they underwent the struggle of life in the wilderness, they began to complain to God. Numbers 11 states how God heard them and became so angry that the fire from Him began to burn the people. As the Israelites saw this, they cried out to Moses for help, who prayed; and the fire died down. However, this behavior took place repeatedly. God provided the heavenly manna for them, but they still acted ungratefully. They did not look at what God was doing for them but instead focused on their material needs.

Some foreigners among the Israelites had an intense craving for other kinds of food. Even the Israelites started crying again, saying, "Now the mixed multitude who were among them yielded to intense craving; so the children of Israel also wept again and said: "Who will give us meat to eat? We remember the fish which we ate freely in Egypt, the cucumbers, the melons, the leeks, the onions, and the garlic; but now our whole being is dried up; there is nothing at all except this manna before our eyes!" (Numbers 11:4–6 NKJV).

The Israelites did not make their requests known to God with an attitude of faith. Instead, they grumbled about how they were tired of consuming the manna, completely overlooking that God had at least not left them for dead in the wilderness. Their behavior is no different from how we act when things are not going our way. No matter how many blessings God gives us, we complain, even if He does not fulfill our wishes only once. We begin to protest and worry. We become anxious and start creating negative scenarios in our heads. That implies that we are only belittling God's ability to make provisions for us. We are looking at our present circumstances and undermining what God can do for us.

Through the passage in the Gospel of Luke, Jesus wants us to understand that if there is anything that can alter our circumstances, it is God's power. Our attitude of worries cannot bring the slightest change. That is why He wants us to shift our focus from worry toward His kingdom. He wants us to believe that even though we cannot see His blessings in the physical realm, they are already sealed in the heavenly realms on our behalf and will be manifested in due time.

That is what Paul talks about in 2 Corinthians 4:17 (NKJV): "For our light affliction, which is but for a moment, is working for us a far more exceeding and eternal weight of glory, while we do not look at the things which are seen, but at the things which are not seen. For the things which are seen are temporary, but the things which are not seen are eternal."

Whether it is sickness, financial debt, a problem at the workplace, a troubled relationship, or any other affliction, they are just momentary tribulations that will pass away. However, what will remain is the kingdom of God and our preordained blessings in heaven. These are eternal, which is why we need to fix our eyes on them and not worry about the fleeting situations of life. Now, this does not mean we stop focusing on our life's responsibilities just because we have been commanded to focus on the eternal. Jesus wants us to follow Him because we receive power and authority through His Spirit at work within us when we do that. When we spend more time praying and reading God's Word, we unlock our blessings in the supernatural realms.

Moreover, we receive authority over our circumstances because of our faith. In Mark 11:23 (NKJV), Jesus says, "For assuredly, I say to you, whoever says to this mountain, 'Be removed and be cast into the sea,' and does not doubt in his heart, but believes that those things he says will be done, he will have whatever he says."

Doubt and worry go hand in hand and are the ultimate nemeses of faith. Jesus teaches us that when we replace that feeling of uncertainty and worry with faith, we gain more control over our circumstances. By faith, we can wait and put our trust in Him. As we declare faith, He manifests His spiritual blessings in our physical world.

My wife and I have had several experiences in life where troubles encompassed us, and we thought we had no option but to worry and feel helpless. However, as we held fast to our faith in God and prayed over our circumstances, we saw our situations change through the power of His Spirit.

A miracle that comes to us is often attached to our obedience because, through obedience, the Lord wants to deliver us from a situation. If we worry, we only allow ourselves to be clouded by weariness. We keep harboring negative thoughts and belittle God's ability to make provisions for us. That is why holding on to our faith with obedience is essential. No matter what we go through, we need to wait on the Lord, knowing that even though we cannot see our miracle right now, it is right around the corner.

In Matthew 14, we see a supernatural miracle. Since the people followed Him from every area, He had many followers around Him. The Bible says that in a remote place, the people met Him, and He healed those who were sick. The people were hungry, and the disciples came to Jesus and told Him that He should send the crowd away. But Jesus said, "No, I'm not going to send a crowd back. You all will give them something to eat."

The disciples wondered, "What does He mean by telling us to give them something?" The disciples said to Jesus, "We only have five loaves of bread and two fish here."

Jesus told them to bring them to Him. He directed the people to sit down. You see, He told them to sit down or rest. It depicts that before there is a supernatural provision in our lives, we must be at a place of rest. Jesus took the five loaves and two fish, looked to heaven, and thanked God. That was true worship. He might have prayed something like "God, I thank You for this little food. Though it is not much, I believe you will multiply this little one." The Bible says that Jesus gave thanks irrespective of the quantity of the resources. However, because of the mercy of the Lord, there was multiplication. Five thousand and above were fed with five loaves of bread and two fish. If He could do it then, He could still do it now. I encourage you to invest in His presence. Believe in Him. Don't live a life of worry, and you will enjoy the supernatural provision and guidance into wealth from the Lord.

Have this attitude of faith even when the devil creates situations around us where it is easier to worry. Jesus wants us to keep praying, not out of doubt and anxiousness but with a firm belief that He has already sealed our blessings in heaven. As we start living our lives from the inside out, translating our positivity and spirituality into our daily lives, the atmosphere of worry will disappear. We will only be surrounded by the presence of the Spirit of God, and He will reveal to us the tremendous hidden treasures He has in store.

When faced with chaos, don't fear or worry. Seek God and praise Him from the place of rest, and heaven will open, and divine strategy from the Holy Spirit will produce supernatural wisdom and divine provision.

Following is a testimony that I pray will bless you. My wife and my son moved to be with me in Indiana. During this period, we were going through a lot of tough situations. My wife had a part-time job, and along with that part-time job, all she brought in a month was a thousand dollars. I was in school full-time and made no income, so our total income was about $1,000 and some change.

In this amount, we had to pay our apartment rent, which was $675 a month. Apart from that, we had a car loan of $350 a month and car insurance of an additional $150. Of course, we had bills to pay too and had to shop for groceries. Calculate the math! All income was totally used, and nothing was left. You can imagine how funny this is.

However, there is one thing we always did: whenever that money came in, we removed our tithe and offerings and then used whatever was left. When we did this, God supernaturally provided for us. I will never forget the day I returned from school, and my wife told me there was no food in the house. We opened the fridge, and it was empty. There was nothing. Our boy was just a few months old then. My wife and I will forever remember our encounter with the Lord, where He said that we didn't need to worry. So what did we do? We checked the bank account, and it was zero. However, we still left the house, prayed to the Lord, and went to the store. We entered the store, filled our cart with groceries, and approached the cashier. We took out the bank card, gave it to the cashier, and held our breaths while the cashier swiped the bank card. To our relief, it worked! We were amazed the card went through. We began to praise the Lord with a dance, heading out of the store to the car. When we went home and checked the bank account, it was still on zero and no negative.

We ate the food. It took us about a week and a few days. We checked the account several times, but it still stayed at zero.

The food was consumed! We had not yet received any money—nothing!

My wife and I said, "OK, we're going to go back again," so we went back to the store. This time, we took two carts. We filled them up to the brim, went to the cashier, and gave them the card to swipe.

Glory to God! The card went through.

We worshipped the Lord as we went to the car with a dance. We went back home and checked the account; it was still zero. That is a supernatural provision from God.

He knows our needs; if we focus on Him, He focuses on us. If we don't worry and rely on Him, we will experience His supernatural provision.

Another testimony is from when I left Maryland to go to Indiana. My wife and son stayed in Maryland, waiting for the transition until they could join me in Indiana. I got to Indiana with just $20 in my pocket and my high hopes. I went to church every Sunday and had nothing in the house for the first few weeks. During this time, I needed money to get books for my school. I did not have enough money to get even a single book, and I was honestly worried about the situation.

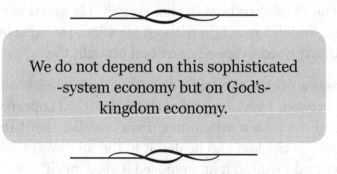

We do not depend on this sophisticated -system economy but on God's- kingdom economy.

However, something awesome happened in the church I regularly visited as I had just arrived. As a matter of fact, I was the only black brother in the congregation. One Sunday after the service, the pastor called me in for a talk to get to know me more. I told him I was there for school. This was before the Sunday service started. In the middle of the service, he called me to stand up, and he told the church to contribute and assist with my studies. They gave me money that was enough to buy two main books. I attended this church twice, and they did that—a very loving congregation. Bill Rooker, an awesome pastor, just went to be with the Lord.

Then, one day, after returning from school, I was starving; and when I reached home, I explored the fridge and found cooked chicken in the refrigerator.

I called my wife and said, "Honey, I'm famished, and I don't know what to do. I don't even have a microwave to heat the chicken."

She replied to me, saying, "Honey, I want you to do it traditionally."

I asked, "OK, how?"

She said, "Take a pot, put some water in it, and heat it. Then wrap the chicken and place it inside."

I complied. While I was heating the water, I got a phone call from one of the brothers in that church. He asked me for my address, which I gave him without question. He came by, and I was so surprised to see what he had brought me.

It was a microwave and a computer desk table, both things that I needed. I was beyond ecstatic that God supernaturally provided me with a microwave. I was so glad that I instantly took out the chicken and heated it in the microwave. Then the brother and I shared it and enjoyed it very much.

It was a beautiful evening with plentiful food and talks about God's gloriousness. We laughed together, overjoyed in His provision.

God can supernaturally provide when you are in need. Now, my brother brought the things I desperately needed, which were a great blessing when I got them. God knew the perfect timing for me to receive them, and He made it happen.

Then, sometime later, it was time for me to buy more books for my course. As always, the Lord provided. My younger brother gave me his credit card to use as I saw fit. I couldn't have been more thankful as he told me to get whatever I wanted with it. The Lord supernaturally provided my books, groceries, and other necessities.

For that season, I appreciate my parents and my family. They played a massive role in helping us out during a difficult time while we were settling in Indiana. That was all supernatural provision from the Lord.

5

❖

Your Authority

WHen God created human beings, He fashioned them in His image, giving them His attributes and a share in His authority. Then God blessed them and said to them, "Be fruitful and multiply; fill the earth and subdue it; have dominion over the fish of the sea, over the birds of the air, and over every living thing that moves on the earth" (Genesis 1:28 NKJV).

Since the beginning of the universe, God's authority has been visible in all He created. He spoke the Word; and the syllables that came out of His mouth formed the sky, sun, moon, stars, land, water, vegetation, and every living creature to inhabit it. At His word, all creation bowed and obeyed. However, when God created humans, He added a unique substance to them, which set them apart from the rest of the creation. He exalted them and increased their value. They were His image.

As the Lord made them, He did not just spill out His creativity like an artist on a canvas. All the other things He had made were sufficient to testify to His craftsmanship and creativity. However, humans were a form of self-expression for Him. He had sculpted them with His hands, delighting in them; and finally, He breathed His breath into their nostrils, adding life to their clay bodies. They embodied His grace, love, holiness, and purity. They had all the qualities of God. This unique privilege gave them superiority and authority over all created things. Therefore, God told them to subdue the earth and multiply so that as they grew in number, the image of God would also spread across the globe.

Now, this is where the crafty enemy showed up and tried to destroy the plan of God. The Bible tells us how jealousy had initially caused him to disobey God. Because of his rebellious nature, he had been thrown out of the kingdom of God. Since then, his goal has been to usurp God's authority and take on His sovereignty. When God created humans in His image, it became the devil's goal to stop that plan from being executed. Thus, he entered the scene and convinced Adam and Eve to disobey God by eating from the forbidden tree. With his cunning speech, he enticed them and then successfully lured them into sinning against God. What seemed like a temporary effect of one act of disobedience resulted in a lifelong banishment from the presence of God. In particular, they were deprived of the image of God. The devil had succeeded. The image of God given to man was made distorted and sinful. However, while hopelessness surfaced over the Bible story and the enemy rejoiced, God soon sent His Son to redeem the people from the power of sin and restore that lost image of God in humanity. He came and removed all barriers that sin had brought in and instead gave them a chance to regain that lost image by believing and having faith in Him. Today, by faith in Christ, we have the image of God in us, and this is our identity. It gives us authority over our circumstances and removes all timidity, fear, doubt, and worry. It is no wonder that the devil is actively working toward destroying that image again. He may work differently today than in that era, but his efforts are visible in everything around us.

As Christians, we are surrounded by various challenges, such as media, television, social gatherings, societal norms, values, etc. All these things convince us to be someone we are not. Different standards of beauty, purity, and personalities always attack our identities in Christ. The devil has laid his trap so that we find his crafty schemes woven into everything, and this seems almost inescapable.

The influence of sin is so great over the world that it is likely to make us question who we are. There is no doubt that many of us do this. We overthink ourselves; compare ourselves to others; and undermine our talents, skills, and qualities. As a result, we develop insecurities and forget what God wants us to be. This is the devil's most significant victory. That is why, as a believer in Christ, the most important thing is to recognize the image of God in us and His authority. We need to know who we are and what God has deposited in us so that the world's lies may never succeed in making us feel otherwise. That is for every believer, both the congregation and those in authority, like pastors, apostles, and bishops. It is for every born-again Christian. If you have come to the revelation of the love of Jesus and have become His disciple, then you are a representative of heaven here on earth to bear His image. You must make Him known in a world that doesn't recognize Him. That is what Jesus reminded the disciples when He gave them the great commission, saying, "All authority has been given to Me in heaven and on earth. Go therefore and make disciples of all the nations, baptizing them in the name of the Father and of the Son and the Holy Spirit, teaching them to observe all things that I have commanded you; and lo, I am with you always, even to the end of the age" (Matthew 28:18–20 NKJV). Amen.

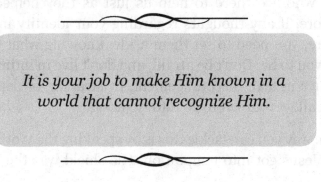

It is your job to make Him known in a world that cannot recognize Him.

As Jesus gave His final instructions to the disciples, He reminded them of the authority that God had given them. By this, He meant His power, sovereignty, and the image He bore of the Father. At the time when Jesus came, the world had no hope for salvation. They looked forward to a Messiah who would save them, but according to their standards, the Messiah had not come. However, as Jesus came, He embodied in Himself all the characteristics and attributes of the Lord. That might not have qualified for a Messiah to the world. Still, these characteristics were the exact image of the Father. Jesus also talked about this on one occasion in John 14:9 (NKJV), "Have I been with you so long, and yet you have not known Me, Philip? He who has seen Me has seen the Father; so how can you say, 'Show us the Father?'"

In response to the disciples' curiosity to see God the Father, Jesus let them know He was the self-expression and a perfect representation of the Father. Thus, His authority remained with Him. When He went out to preach, He performed miracles and wonders, and the angels of the Lord continually ministered to Him. He was strong, courageous, and unbothered by the criticism and hatred of the people because He recognized His authority and position.

Jesus's example tells us what life would look like if we start recognizing our identities too. The angels of the Lord have been assigned to walk with us and to help us. They are ministering spirits who are there to help us just as they helped Jesus. Therefore, if any thoughts regarding your identity make you insecure, you need to set them aside, knowing what God has called you to be. Don't be afraid, and don't live in intimidation. Don't live in fear, discouragement, frustration, or depression. Do not allow yourself to go into isolation.

One way you can tackle this is by speaking the Word of God. When Jesus got into temptation, His shield was the Word of

God to rebuke the devil. Similarly, when the devil comes to you and makes you have doubts and insecurities about yourself, you need to embrace the Word of God and use it as your weapon. The Bible says, "Let the weak say I am strong. Let the poor say I am rich." The devil may be troubling you with thoughts of deprivation or failure. You may not have a car right now, and you may not even have a bicycle, but you may have your legs. With the help of those legs, you walk and go to church. If people laugh at you, all you need to do is hear the small voice of the Holy Spirit inside you that reminds you that everything is possible and your dreams will come true.

Speak to yourself that you are wealthy and you have what you want. Speak out loud what you want to see in your life; as you do that, you will see God working mightily in your life. God will bless you according to your faith; you need to be happy and content with your identity and rejoice in knowing that God will reveal Himself to you even if you are at your darkest. A revelation will soon occur, and God's glory will descend upon you.

And when God's glory descends, there will be more incredible things than you can imagine.

First Kings 17:1 (NKJV) states, "And Elijah the Tishbite, of the inhabitants of Gilead, said to Ahab, "As the Lord God of Israel lives, before whom I stand, there shall not be dew nor rain these years, except at my word."

Elijah used *except at my word* as a declaration of faith. He showed that he had authority, not because he considered himself more powerful than God but because he recognized the power and authority *of* God. He knew that through God, he had been granted the same authority. Therefore, because he knew the Holy Spirit rested upon him, he could boldly proclaim aloud, and it would happen when He spoke. When the glory comes upon you, what would take you one year will take you one month. You may only need one week to do what would take you one month. What would take you one week, you may accomplish in one day. What would take you one day may just take an hour.

What would take you one hour will take you one minute. What would take you one minute will take you one second. What would take you one second? You will be surrounded by glory. You will be in a place of rest and serenity, just like Elijah did. Elijah knew who he was. He knew he was an ambassador of heaven, and his citizenship was of the eternal home and not here on earth. He did not let fear, doubt, and worry hold him back.

That is why we need to know who we are. When you know who you are and speak God's Word, you will come into a place of rest. Also, God will give you a divine strategy and a way of escaping every situation, even if you are confused and seek the Holy Spirit. You seek God the Father, God the Son, and God the Holy Ghost. He would give you His divine revelation and give you answers that will point you in the right direction.

Proverbs 3:5–5 (NKJV) states, "Trust in the Lord with all your heart, and do not lean on your understanding. In all your ways, acknowledge Him, and He will make straight your paths."

Moses followed a route that would have led them into the Promised Land without going through the waters.

But the Bible says in 1 Corinthians 1:25 (NKJV), "Because the foolishness of God is wiser than men, and the weakness of God is stronger than men."

And so, God had His plan in His mind. The Bible says that on their way, the Lord spoke to Moses and asked him to make a U-turn to go in another direction. And the Lord took them through a path whereby in front of them was the sea, and behind them were the Egyptians coming. They could not go forward or backward and were stuck until God assisted them.

Sometimes, God will divert you in life because He wants to show His power on your behalf. He wants to make your enemies know that you serve a great and living God. He loves demonstrating His power and wants all the glory to be given to Him. As humans, we often do not give Him the glory but try to work according to our wisdom. However, the Lord wants us to recognize and acknowledge His authority. By doing so, we recognize our authority through His power.

The people in the wilderness cried, "Moses, have you taken us out so far from Egypt to kill us? You should have left us in Egypt." As the whining, complaining, and mumbling continued, Moses cried to God, and God answered him and attended to his needs. Moses knew that God had given him power through His staff, yet he completely ignored it and cried out, pressured by the Israelites' complaints. He forgot that the power and authority already belonged to him.

Most of the time, troubles and difficulties are God's way of reminding us of our own identities, which we often forget when we come under pressure. We know that we have power and authority over anything if we pray in His name, yet we often cry out of worry and complaints.

God wants us to know who we are in Him. He wants us to know that our worth is not in material things, physical strength, or money but in what He has placed inside us. He even changes our plans sometimes to make us self-aware. That is because He wants us to be connected to that core part of our existence so that the devil cannot snatch it away from us in any way. And so we may stay true to the image that God has given each one of us individually.

We can command our situation to turn into what God desires it to be, and it will happen. By faith, we can ask for healing, and we will receive it. By faith, we can ask for freedom from financial debt, and it will happen. All we need to do is to believe in His power and let the feeling of worry go. The Holy Spirit is always present with us. Take authority in your praise and see God do wonders for you.

6

❖

Heavenly Treasures

Since the beginning of the world, human beings have chosen to tie their happiness to earthly things. We have drifted away from the pure joy that is available only in God. It all started with the first choice that Adam and Eve made. They disobeyed God just so that they could eat from the forbidden tree. They had access to every good, and yet they chose to disobey Him. He had made everything subject to them, and above all, they had the presence and fellowship of the Lord. Despite this, they decided to eat from the one forbidden tree.

Genesis 3:6 (NKJV) states, "So when the woman saw that the tree was good for food, that it was pleasant to the eyes, and a tree desirable to make one wise, she took off its fruit and ate. She also gave to her husband with her, and he ate."

The above verse shows that there must be something different about the tree that enticed them. Eve saw that its fruit was flavorful and even looked attractive. More importantly, they believed that the most significant advantage was gaining wisdom and knowledge by eating from the tree.

They immediately forgot that there was a tremendous blessing they would have to leave behind if they made this choice. They still went ahead and gave it a shot; they failed to discern what was necessary for their happiness. At that moment, it must have seemed like the forbidden fruit would give them an unforgettable experience. They mistakenly thought that they would achieve greater blessings through it. When the veil was pulled from their eyes, they realized that the happiness they gained from their disobedience was, at best, counterfeit.

It cursed them, which led to their banishment from the presence of God.

Humans have continued to run after temporary happiness only to realize that it didn't bring them joy. I am sure each one of us can relate to this. At some point in our lives, we all have run after fleeting happiness; or as kids, we longed for things that were not beneficial for us. Back in the day, when our parents strictly warned us not to do things we thought gave us joy, we believed they hated us or deprived us of what we needed. However, as we grew up, we understood that they loved us and desired the best for us. Our relationship with God is not very different. He is our Father, our Provider, and our Sustainer. He gives all that we have. James 1:17 (NKJV) states, "Every good gift and every perfect gift is from above, and comes down from the Father of lights, with whom there is no variation or shadow of turning."

His blessings are eternal. When He blesses, He leaves no trace of sorrow in it. However, as human beings, we do not comprehend this truth. Adam and Eve also failed to fathom the depth of His love and grace; therefore, they gave up their eternal treasure for counterfeit joy. They chose mediocrity over greatness and did not understand this until they suffered the consequences.

Today, this habit has taken root in our daily lives. With life racing at such a fast pace, we have so many goals to accomplish. We have set standards for ourselves, whether it is about our career or lifestyle. We do everything possible to grab opportunities as quickly as we can. Especially with the rise of media, our desires have become much stronger. The advertisements on television are forever enticing us to buy new things. There are new inventions and advancements now and then, and before we settle our minds on one thing, there is another to distract us. Life has become all about material things, price tags, and brands. We have started weighing everything according to its material value.

While these things effectively appeal to our eyes, they will not last for very long, and neither are they meant to give any benefit to our souls. First John 2:16 (NKJV) says, "For all that is in the world—the lust of the flesh, the lust of the eyes, and the pride of life—is not of the Father but is of the world."

Notice that John is not merely stating the things that lure us to sin and are vain pursuits of life but is hinting at a crucial part of the whole Bible story—the place where this longing began, where sin first took place. John talks about three things: the lust of the flesh, the lust of the eyes, and the pride of life. Now, look back at what happened in the Garden of Eden. When Adam and Eve committed that sin, three factors attracted them to the fruit. These are

- the tree was good for food,
- the tree was pleasant to the eyes, and
- the tree could make one wise.

In our present world, everything that we see is another tree standing in the Garden of Eden. When John says the lust of the flesh, he refers to how the first human beings considered the tree's fruit nutritious for their bodies. When he says the lust of eyes, he tells us how the fruit was also pleasant to the eyes. When he says the pride of life, the fruit also gave the person the self-sufficiency that man thought he needed.

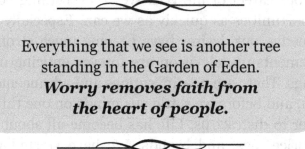

Everything that we see is another tree standing in the Garden of Eden. *Worry removes faith from the heart of people.*

However, while all these things seemed good to Adam and Eve, they ended up bringing them under the curse. What looked good was not right in reality. Similarly, in today's world, we have many things that seem suitable for the body because they make us feel good. They seem appealing to the eye and attract us. Some things promise us success and a bright future. In reality, they are just as devastating for our souls as the fruit of that tree. They may give us a sense of accomplishment and contentment, but this will not last forever.

While Jesus was in the wilderness, He also faced temptation in the three areas mentioned above. In the first temptation in Matthew 4:3 (NKJV), Satan said to Jesus, "If You are the Son of God, command that these stones become bread." But He answered, "It is written, 'Man shall not live by bread alone, but by every word that proceeds from the mouth of God.'" Satan first tempted Him regarding His physical needs. The enemy knew that the Lord had been fasting, so he brought Him this offer.

In the second temptation in Matthew 4:6 (NKJV), Satan said, "If You are the Son of God, throw Yourself down. For it is written: 'He shall give His angels charge over you," and "In their hands, they shall bear you up, lest you dash your foot against a stone.'"

This offer questioned His authority and power and tried to test it. But Jesus once again used the Word of God, saying, "It is written again, 'You shall not tempt the Lord your God.'"

Next, Satan tried for the final time to entice Jesus with the riches of the world. These things were indeed pleasing to the eye. He said in Matthew 4:9–10 (NKJV), "All these things I will give You if You fall down and worship me." But Jesus replied, "Away with you, Satan! For it is written, 'You shall worship the Lord your God, and Him only you shall serve." Jesus, being Human and prone to the sinful nature of the flesh, knew how a man could be tempted. That is why Jesus said in Matthew 6:33 (NKJV), "But seek first the kingdom of God and His righteousness, and all these things shall be added to you."

Jesus wants us to know that everything is available to us in the invisible realm. We do not need to chase after the worldly things that Satan presents to us. He does not want us to be poor on earth while we wait to get to heaven. Instead, He wants us to make Him the source of all good things in our present lives. Therefore, He seeks to shift our focus from the earthly blessings and gives us a new direction in Matthew 6:19–21 (NKJV), "Do not lay up for yourselves treasures on earth, where moth and rust destroy and where thieves break in and steal, but lay up for yourselves treasures in heaven, where neither moth nor rust destroys and where thieves do not break in and steal. For where your treasure is, there your heart will be also."

Like a good parent who lovingly holds back harmful things from a child, Jesus warns us against earthly blessings' futility. However, while He tells us this, He asks us to focus on the heavenly blessings the Father has prepared for Him. He is a good father who knows how to provide and wants the best for us.

Ephesians 1:3–4 (NKJV) states, "Blessed be the God and Father of our Lord Jesus Christ, who has blessed us in Christ with every spiritual blessing in the heavenly places, even as he chose us in him before the foundation of the world, that we should be holy and blameless before him."

The above verse gives us a more in-depth insight into these heavenly blessings. It tells us that our spiritual blessings have been kept in heaven, just like we were chosen before the world was made. That means that nothing given to us results from our toil or a stroke of luck. These are all the results of God's favor, which He bestowed on us before we were even born.

Our unworthiness in our own eyes does not determine the range of God's blessings. He blesses according to His promises, and it is not because we have anything good or deserving in ourselves. God's unfailing compassion and mercy wipe away our sinfulness and qualify us to access His throne of grace, where He blesses everyone generously.

One night, after spending time in prayers, I went to bed, and I had a dream that felt so real. In this dream, I approached a door in this beautiful place. The color of the door was kind of dark red, with nice wood all around—very beautifully shaped and attractive. I noticed I was being escorted toward the door. When we got to this door, it opened; and to my amazement, I saw things I had never seen here on earth. I stood looking at everything and the activities taking place. I felt so unholy and looking for a place to hide. As I stood there, the atmosphere was so holy, pure, and joyful. I have no words to explain this feeling. In this huge warehouse, I saw angelic beings all dressed in the most beautiful gold attire. Some had wings, and others did not. I tell you the truth that they were extremely beautiful and covered in gold.

I saw extremely beautiful chandeliers of various sizes and decors in gold. While I was standing, an angelic being walked toward me and told me to sit. I was just gazing in amazement over what I was seeing and the activities taking place. I was afraid to sit, but this angel insisted that I sit down. I sat down, still making sure I stained nothing. I felt so unworthy to be in such an atmosphere of purity. While sitting, I saw these angelic beings come and go. They would pick one thing, and immediately, they would disappear. I saw jewelry covered in sparkling pure gold, and in my mind, I said, *Wow, that would be good for my wife.*

Immediately, as that thought came to mind, one huge angelic being walked over to me and said, "Take as many as you want for her." Then he said, "This is a treasure house for the saints." When we pray, they are assigned to get from this storehouse and deliver to earth. I left with some things for my wife. At this time, I was descending, and I woke up. I shared my dream with my wife and prophetically delivered the blessings to her. I wish it could have manifested physically. Everything we need is available in the treasure warehouse, which is in heaven, and God loves to deliver it to us in any form.

Some people have testified about seeing a storehouse in heaven full of body parts available to those who seek a creative miracle. Anything we need is available in the treasure house! Why worry? Communicate to your Father in heaven, the creator of the universe, in a place of rest, praise, and worship and see the great assistance of God himself.

Even though we have blessings stored in heaven, we still have to pray and gain access to the spiritual realm to allow those blessings to manifest. Many of us who come to the Lord think that believing and repenting will turn our lives upside down. We will be flooded with blessings, and all our problems will be taken away. However, following Christ does not mean that life's difficulties will not meet us along the way. These are inevitable. However, God does promise us blessings and favor amid these troubles that we can access when we get into close fellowship with Him.

Our unworthiness in our own eyes
does not determine the range
of God's blessings

Second Corinthians 4:17–18 (NKJV) states, "For our light affliction, which is but for a moment, is working for us a far more exceeding and eternal weight of glory, while we do not look at the things which are seen, but at the things which are not seen. For the things which are seen are temporary, but the things which are not seen are eternal."

Thus, we must seek our treasures in heaven. We must shift our gaze from earthly things to spiritual treasures because they will last forever. We need to gain this through the supernatural; but we also need to understand that we have to let go of worry, discouragement, and fear to achieve that.

Worry was an obstacle for Israel, which hindered them from making it into the Promised Land. If you recall the miracles that God did for them, can you imagine the Israelites abandoning their many treasures when they left Egypt? Moreover, the Lord praised their sacrifice; when He parted the Red Sea for them to walk through, the Lord destroyed their enemies.

Among all this, the Bible clarifies that the clothes were clean and in excellent condition. It is truly a miracle that God made sure that their clothes were clean and that nothing terrible or impure touched them, even in the wilderness. It shows the extent of God's blessings of how much the Lord cared for the people and how He not only protected the bodies of the people but did not let their clothes and shoes be ruined.

They wore the same shoes for almost forty years. Moreover, heaven was opened, and God provided heavenly manna for food. Despite this, they were worried, complained, and could not get into the Promised Land. Moses could only see, but he could not enter. I pray that you will not only see but come and experience what God has for you. God wants you to experience Him supernaturally, for He's a supernatural God who provides for His children.

7

━━━━◈◈◈━━━━

Destiny Helpers

Now if God so clothes the grass of the field, which
today is, and tomorrow is thrown into the oven, will
He not much more clothe you, O you of little faith?

—Matthew 6:30 (NKJV)

Before anything manifests in the physical, its victory takes place in the spiritual realm. If you are a Christian, you must believe in angels. If you don't believe in angels as a Christian, then you are not a Christian. Why? Because Jesus believed in angels. First, they are creatures, which means they were created. Whatever God created must be sustained by God. We are not told the exact time of their creation, but we know they existed long before man appeared. If you will live a life of no worry, God has your back. As mentioned in the scripture above, "Will he not clothe you O you of little faith?" In other words, God will release destiny helpers to assist you in every endeavor if you don't lose faith. Thus, the primary purpose of these destiny helpers is to bring the plan of God to completion. If God wants to fulfill His plan, He will use all means possible or impossible to make it happen. All we must do is to be strong in faith.

The angel of the Lord encamps all around those who fear Him, and delivers them. (Psalm 34:7 NKJV)

You remember the story of Elisha waking up in the morning; there was an army of thousands of soldiers coming to capture him because, by the Spirit of God, Elisha was capable of hearing whatever the king of Syria would say in his inner chamber against Israel. I can imagine the servant of Elisha going out in the morning to use the bathroom. As he opened the door, he saw an army in great numbers surrounding the house. He immediately rushed back in with a shout and in great fear and worry. The servant knew the end was near, fearing that they were dead today. Elisha was very calm and relaxed despite seeing an army of horses, spears, and daggers all around. Elijah was so calm, yet his servant was so scared. The master said, "Don't worry about it. We're safe."

The son, the servant, said, "But, master, what do you mean we're safe? We're going to be killed."

Elisha said, "O Lord, open his eyes that he may see."

The Bible calls this group he saw heavenly hosts. Now, *hosts* means "plenty" or "uncountable." And the Bible says, "And Elisha prayed, and said, 'LORD, I pray, open his eyes that he may see.' Then the LORD opened the eyes of the young man, and he saw. And behold, the mountain was full of horses and chariots of fire all around Elisha" (2 Kings 6:17 NKJV). After the servant saw these angelic warriors, I can imagine that he boldly opened the door to head to the bathroom.

Elisha knew he was an ambassador of heaven here on earth. With authority in him, Elisha commanded blindness on the Syrian army, and they were all blind. I firmly believe that as you focus on Jesus Christ, He will open your eyes to see and experience the heavenly angelic realm around you. There's more activity going on above your head and below your feet.

Sometimes you feel alone. If you only knew who was with and who was for you, you would start dancing right now. The problem is, if you don't recognize who you are in Christ Jesus, even though the angels are made available, you can't put them to work. See, around us, there are angelic beings. They are always moving in our midst with lightning speed and noiseless movement. They pass from place to place instantly.

There is a famous adage that goes, "Whatever is meant to be will be." It hints toward the powerful force of destiny helpers. It shows us the perspective that, eventually, everything is going to fall into place. While some embrace this as a motivation to keep going on in life despite the difficulties, others may use it as an excuse to continue in passiveness. There may still be some who simply view the whole concept through the lens of unbelief and skepticism. Thus, the primary purpose of these destiny helpers is to bring the plan of God to completion. We may not always be the ones who are given the task to accomplish alone. If God wants to fulfill His plan, He will use all means possible or impossible to make it happen. All we must do is to be strong in faith.

What a privilege to know that the angels of God are always in great numbers around those who fear God. The fear of God here is a reference to reverence, respect, right standing, and honor. In other words, if we put God as our priority in every area of our lives, we will very much benefit from His angelic beings assigned to help and minister to us here on earth. When the angels of God encamp around you, there's no place for worry. The angels of God are known to be ministering spirits. Hebrews 1:14 (NKJV) says, "Are they not all ministering spirits sent forth to minister for those who will inherit salvation?"

> "The primary purpose of these destiny
> helpers is to bring the plan of
> God to completion."

ANGELIC DIVINE INTERVENTION

Growing up, I used to walk around our home in the night, and I would even go outside to look up in the skies to see if I could see an angel coming down. My anticipation of experiencing the realm of heaven around me was high. As previously stated, my wife and I, with our children, are privileged to have encounters with Jesus Christ and the heavenly realm. Let me share with you a marvelous testimony of divine intervention and how the angels of God go before us.

My family and I were preparing to move to Ashtabula, Ohio, to pastor a church there. When we arrived, the first question we asked the Lord was if it was promotion or demotion because it's so rural and laid-back. We could hardly find a more decent home. On our last trip to search, my wife said, "If we can't find a good place to live, then it's not God's will."

I said, "OK."

We drove around with the pastor emeritus and wife for several hours and were at the point of giving up. Just at the point of giving up, the pastor's wife saw an advertisement to purchase condominiums or build. We called, and the builder said there's one home available, but the owner intends to use it as a vacation or retirement complex. We said we needed a place to rent. The builder in charge told us to come with him while he got in touch with the owner. When we saw the three-bedroom first-floor single condominium, it was lovely and comfortable. We loved it and sat on the floor, waiting for the owner. The owner arrived. He was an elderly gentleman. Looking at us, the owner said he liked us and changed his mind about moving there. He then asked us to name a price to rent. We were astonished at the question. We gave him what we could afford at the time; it was way less than its value. Surprisingly, he immediately said, "Yes, move in." We were so excited and praised God for such a miracle! The angels of the Lord were at work, and God did it for us.

The elderly couple was so gracious to us. They loved us dearly. By God's grace, we ministered the gospel to them; they gave their lives to Jesus Christ and attended church as their strength permitted. They gave to the ministry and were a great blessing. A time came when the elderly father was hospitalized. We would regularly visit, read the Bible, and pray with the elderly couple. However, he passed. When this happened, we were told to move from the condominium. We did not know where to go with such short notice.

One night, as we prayed and went to bed, my wife had a dream. The Holy Spirit revealed to my wife a personal issue concerning the brother of the building project manager for the condominium. I encouraged my wife to call and inform him. She did, and this project manager was so shocked and asked if my wife was a psychic. Everything my wife told him was true and came to pass. Praise God! My wife went to see the brother to pray for him.

It was so funny that this project manager would ask my wife questions about his life and family. My wife kept saying she was a woman of God, and God would speak through her. Soon, the project manager started visiting the church and was led to Jesus Christ. As a matter of fact, he was the one who came and told us that the owner's family wanted us out. He felt so bad and went the extra mile to talk with one of his brothers to rent us his home on the other side of town. His brother agreed to rent his home to us while he moved to Florida. This project manager told us that as long as we were at his brother's, he would come to plow the snow all season and cut the grass for us without charges. He did it faithfully while his brother decided to pay $300 a month toward our rent. We did not worry about the snow plowing so long as we stayed there, plus they assisted us with the rent payment. Wow! That's the favor of God, and the angels of God were at work.

As our time for staying at this house was coming to a close, we were given the option to purchase the home. We had no intention of purchasing the house, so we were given six months' notice to leave. While staying there, we were told it'd been sold, and we had to move. Again, we looked around and found no place to go. My wife and I prayerfully decided to buy a house. I wasn't ready to buy until my wife approached me and said, "Let's try." We did try and were surprisingly approved for the loan, but it could not get us into the house we loved because it was a small loan. My wife and I would search a particular area online, and this one house kept popping up. We asked our real estate agent to see it, but the Realtor politely discouraged us by saying we wouldn't qualify to purchase there. I insisted that we go check. As we got there, we were told we could build a home. The Realtor again tried to talk us out of it, but we insisted. This company assisted us through the process.

We were approved for a three-bedroom home with a basement. When I looked again at the various sizes and model homes, I saw one design that caught my attention. I told my wife that I would request the larger home for the same price. My wife pleaded with me not to try. The sizes and costs were far apart. I told my wife that I would give it a shot. We went back to this office, where I spoke to the representative. She laughed and said it couldn't be done with the loan amount we were approved for. I told the representative to kindly put my request to the owners of the entire building project. The representative did, and to our surprise, the owners accepted the offer. The monthly payment for the gorgeous home was lowered as well. We were told not to mention to anyone what favor they did for us. My wife and I danced and praised God on our way home.

The building came to completion, and we were ready to close and move into our new home in three days. We were told the keys couldn't be given to us until we proved that we had paid the IRS. We did clear all IRS debts. We called the IRS, and they said it would take about ten days to a month to receive that document. The mortgage company tried to intervene, but the IRS refused to fax or email the proof, stating they can't do that; it has never been done that way. My wife and I decided to go into the house. It was open for us to go in.

We stood on the stairways going to the bedrooms and held our hands to pray. After praying, we called the IRS, and they still said no, we must wait. My wife and I praised God and danced, then held our hands again to pray. After praying and dancing for the Lord, we called again, and a lady answered the phone. She asked if we needed a document for the purchase of our home. My wife and I were surprised by the question simply because we did not even say why we were calling. And we said, "YES!"

She gave us her name and said, "I will fax it to you."

I immediately called the mortgage company and had them on a three-way line. This lady at the IRS office faxed that document after they said it couldn't be done. The loan company officer was also surprised because she had been on the phone with them several times and heard the same denial.

As we hung up the phone, we called back and requested the same documents. They told us they wouldn't fax or email them because it's not their policy. Out of curiosity, I asked for the agent who served us. They searched their system for that name and could not find it. We were told there's no one by that name in that office. Wow, do you know what happened? The angel of the Lord got into that office and faxed that document. We moved into our new home in three days as scheduled.

The angels of God are eager to assist us in every area. Why worry or live in fear? Release your angels to work. It's our birthright in Christ Jesus to communicate with our assigned angels from God! The most extraordinary evidence of their existence is the fact that Jesus Christ Himself often spoke about angels. He even referred to them in teaching; he also personally received ministry from them in Matthew 4:11.

Matthew 13:41 (NKJV) says, "The Son of Man will send out his angels and they will weed out of his kingdom, everything that causes sin and all who do evil."

In Mark 13:32 (NKJV), it is recorded, "But of that day and that hour knoweth no man, no, not the angels which are in heaven, neither the Son, but the Father."

Matthew 26:53 (NKJV) says, "Do you not think, I cannot call on my father and even at once put at my disposal more than 12 legions of angels?"

Who was talking to whom? To those who came to arrest him. He said, "I could call my Father right now, and He would send me twelve legions of angels." Now, a legion consists of six thousand soldiers. Jesus said, "My Father could dispatch a small group of seventy-two thousand angels to wipe you out." Jesus Christ was talking about these mighty creatures.

After he was tempted, the Bible says in Matthew 4:11 (AMP), "Then the devil left Him; and angels came and ministered to Him [bringing Him food and serving Him]." The Bible teaches that between God and man is a massive activity of spiritual beings that not every man can see with the physical eye. Around us is a spiritual world far more populous, powerful, and resourceful than Earth. Jesus Christ believed in the existence of angels. Jesus was not expressing a superstitious belief of the people when He said He believed in angels. He did not fail to correct popular opinion in tradition when it was necessary.

Colossians 2:18 (NKJV) says Paul is speaking, "Let no one cheat you of your reward, taking delight in false humility and worship of angels, intruding into those things which he has not seen, vainly puffed up by his fleshly mind."

Paul was correcting the Gnostic theory rampant in the church at Colossae, where people were worshipping angels and calling it part of the gospel. Even today, in some religions, people worship angels. The Bible teaches against the worship of angels. Whether you make a statue of them or wear angelic jewelry, you are not allowed by God's command of any human to worship an angel. The first reason they shouldn't be worshipped is that they are created beings. Anything that God created must not be worshipped. I will repeat: anything that God created must not be worshipped. Jesus said, "Thou shalt worship God and him only shalt thou serve." The word *God* means "existing one." That means that if something doesn't need anything to exist, it qualifies as being God. The angels were created; therefore, they depend on God. The word *create* is the Hebrew word *bara*, which means to "fall from nothing." Angels are disqualified from being worshipped. That is why when Lucifer demanded worship, he had to be removed. He was asking for the impossible. You can't be God unless you can exist by yourself. That's why the first commandment (of the

Ten Commandments) forbids man from worshipping anything except God, whether created beings, animals, or idols. Angels are not departed human spirits. I repeat: angels are not ghosts. An angel is not the spirit of departed or glorified human beings. Colossians 2:18 (NIV) says, "Do not let anyone who delights in false humility and the worship of angels disqualify you for the prize."

We do not worship angels. As you focus on Jesus, that realm opens to you.

The prophet Isaiah wrote about the angels of the Lord in Isaiah 63:9 (NKJV), saying, "In all their affliction, he was afflicted, and the angel of his presence saved them." This is a reference to the angel of the Lord. Obviously, if you look at those verses, two important things about this angel stand out. When it says he has the name of the Lord, it means that he is the Lord. It also says that Jehovah's face may be seen in him. Face implies character and nature. This creature has the face of the Lord, the favor of God, and the grace of God. Jacob identifies him with God himself.

That's why the Bible never refers to the angel of the Lord as being created. I think the word *angel* may be important to clarify. Sometimes it is rendered a heavenly being. In this particular case, the angel of the Lord is rendered that way. In other words, Jesus Christ is from heaven, but He's not an angel, as in the case of the other angels. Whenever He shows up, something tangible happens. Do you remember reading when Joshua first came into Jericho in Joshua 5:13–14 (NKJV)? The Bible says, "And it came to pass, when Joshua was by Jericho, that he lifted his eyes and looked, and behold, a Man stood opposite him with His sword drawn in His hand." Joshua fell on his face and began to worship."

The angel never told him to get up. Now, in every other case where a man bows to an angel, the angel tells him to get up. But when it came to this one, he told the man to stay right there. Why? "I'm worthy of worship." Then, Joshua asked him a question, "Who are you with? Are you with me, or are you with them?"

The man said, "No, but as commander of the army of the Lord, I have come."

In other words, he said, "I have come to bring victory for you. What do you want me to do?"

And Joshua got specific instructions from the Lord. He obeyed the words of the Lord, and the victory was won. This is Christ, the angel of the Lord.

SOME CHARACTERISTICS OF ANGELS

- Angels are not humans; they're creatures.
- They are spirits because, unlike men, they are not limited by physical and natural conditions.
- They are spiritual beings; they appear and disappear at will.
- They travel by unnatural means.
- They are mighty beings. It is very important to note that while angels are powerful, their power is delegated. They don't have power onto themselves; it's given to them by God (Psalm 103:20).
- They are immortal. They are not subject to death.
- Though purely spirits, they also have the power to assume human form and make their presence visible to our senses. That happened several times in the scriptures (Genesis 19:1).
- Angels carry fire. Psalm 104:4 (NKJV) says, "Who makes His angels spirits, His ministers a flaming fire."

By the grace of God, I see them in meetings. These angels collaborate with the Holy Spirit. I often will see liquid fire on the heads of people and tell them. In most cases, they will experience the intense heat and receive a miracle, or they are ignited and on fire for Jesus Christ. Do you want to hear what kind of power the angels of God have? They are called the might of God. One angel rolled the stones that multiple men had to move, and then he sat on them.

- One angel killed the firstborn of Egypt.
- In Isaiah 37:36, one angel of the Lord went out and put to death 185,000 men in the Assyrian camp.
- One angel will take care of Lucifer in Revelation.

You don't need to worry, for God has your back. Whenever there are multiple angelic activities, guess what happens? Archangel Michael and his warriors have to break through the demonic principalities to reach us.

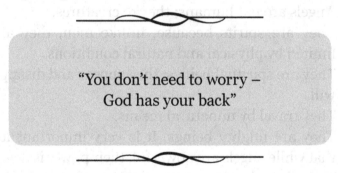

"You don't need to worry –
God has your back"

What Is an Archangel?

Michael is mentioned as the archangel, a chief angel. The English word *archangel* is derived from Greek ἀρχάγγελος, literally "chief" (Freedictionary.com). Archangel means the chief of angels. He was the one put in charge by God over all the warrior angels. Jude 9, Revelation 12:7, and 1 Thessalonians

4:16 mentioned the Archangel Michael. "At that time Michael shall stand up, the great prince who stands watch over the sons of your people" (Daniel 10:21, 12:1 NKJV). He's the one who watches over the nation or the chosen ones of God.

When Daniel's prayer couldn't get through, he prayed in Daniel 10:13 and asked God for His knowledge of things to come. There were some problems in the atmosphere—all kinds of demon powers between heaven and earth. The answer was sent the same day that he prayed, but the demon powers held back the answers from reaching Daniel. It was held up for twenty-one days.

Now, the Bible says Daniel kept on praying. Every day at the same time, Daniel prayed. Why? Because he knew that the answer had to come, the answer already came. I believe Daniel's persistent prayer caused Michael to go into action because the Bible says, "Then the Archangel Michael had to come and fight, to create a clear path for the messenger angel to come down and deliver the message God had for Daniel."

According to Daniel 10:13–14 (NKJV), the angels fight for you to have what you believe to receive from God. You should not give up when things take a while. As a matter of fact, why don't you hang on for 21 days and see what happens? Don't quit because it doesn't happen tomorrow or next week or even the week after. Be like Daniel; remain steadfast until you see the answer.

Archangels are powerful creatures. Gabriel is also seen as an archangel who is entrusted with messages of the highest importance. Whenever God wants to send an important message, He gives it to Gabriel. When God wants critical battles fought and won, He sends Michael. You could say that Michael oversees military operations while Gabriel is in charge of media and communications.

Get ready to receive your answer from God. A messenger angel is on his way to you. Don't worry and don't live in fear or discouragement; your answer or breakthrough will arrive right when you need it!

Resurrection Sunday Angelic Encounter

At church, we had been fasting and praying every first three days of every month for a breakthrough in our lives. It was resurrection Sunday, which made one year of fasting and prayers. The church was full of people during this service. I stood at the pulpit and was preaching on the power of resurrection. As I was in the middle of the message, a young man about six feet tall walked into the sanctuary, wearing well-ironed sky-blue pants and a shirt that looked similar to mine. He had beautiful golden hair and a handsome face. He walked in and sat close to our church bus driver and began listening carefully to the message.

My attention was already drawn to him because of his appearance, but I was more intrigued when I saw his reaction to the sermon. Each time I would preach about the power of the blood of Jesus or mention Christ's name, the man would nod and then put his head down. As the service ended and we had an altar call, the people in the congregation began coming forward to give their lives to God. Then, this man got up from his seat and went through the door. As I watched him go, I immediately called one of the pastors to go after him and tell him that I would like to meet with him. The pastor quickly ran to the door, but he could not find the man. The man in the unique blue pants had disappeared. They were a few seconds apart.

The pastor went around the parking lot and the church building to look for him, but he could not find him. Thus, after the service, I asked the entire church if anyone had invited him. Everyone said it was the first time they had seen a person like him in the city. I was preaching in a small town where most people knew one another, yet none recognized him. He was muscular and tall, and his appearance did not match that of the local residents. My wife and I returned home and talked about it because I was still troubled. We didn't know who this person was because he looked so different from each of us. My curiosity drove me crazy.

As we were caught up in perplexity, I called a man of God named Steven Brooks because the man looked like him. As I was telling him that something strange happened in our service today, he interrupted me, "Oh, Gaius, let me tell you, the angel of breakthrough walked into your service this morning." My wife and I were in shock. The Lord had revealed to Steven everything that had happened because it was not a normal encounter but a supernatural experience.

We then called one of the pastors who had been taking pictures at the service. We asked him for the recording of the service. When we played it, we were left astonished to see that the seat where the man sat was empty. Everyone in the church had seen the man, but the camera showed an empty seat. We were amazed at what God had done in our lives. He had finally answered our prayers. After that divine encounter, everyone at our church began experiencing breakthroughs in their lives. My family and I continued to have breakthroughs while we were at that church. Just as Steven had said, the angel of the breakthrough had been released. After that encounter, we did not experience lack, even in the most difficult moments. The Lord would supernaturally provide for the church and us. There were times that offerings would multiply as our financial team was in the process of counting. There's nothing too hard for our God.

Translation

Angels, our "destiny helpers," are available and ready to assist you. This is your season for a mighty visitation from Jesus Christ. May you find favor in Jesus's name. In these last days, we will experience an increase in angelic visitation, even more than in the Old Testament and with the apostles in the New Testament. Children of God would experience multiple translations with great assistance from the angelic realm. Being translated is simply moving from point A to point B in a split second. It is also known as moving supernaturally across time, the earth, and the heavens for God's purposes and for Him alone to be glorified. Remember Philip, the evangelist? In Acts 8:39, the Lord caught Philip away, and the Eunuch saw him no more. I experienced it personally several times.

Another incident took place when God intervened in our situation and provided a breakthrough using destiny helpers. One day, I was invited to pray at the Trump rally in Geneva, Ohio. My wife had to travel to Maryland, so I took my children along. I prayed, and the rally ended at 10:00 p.m. Exhausted after a long day, my children and I set out for the journey to Maryland. It was a six- to seven-hour journey that we had to complete to reach Maryland to visit my grandparents and attend a meeting hosted by my mom. My wife had already reached my parents' house and rearranged the rooms for our kids to stay there. By the time we left the parking lot, it was a six- to seven-hour drive.

I started driving with worship music on in the car. Suddenly, I noticed that we had traveled almost four hours of the journey instantly. We left at 10:45 p.m., and by 11:30 p.m., we had covered a distance of about four hours; we were at our last break stop, Breeze Wood, four hours from Ashtabula, Ohio. We arrived at my parents' home at about 2:00 a.m.; a trip that should have taken six to seven hours took less than four. None of us could believe what had just happened.

Then, my son Lemuel said, "Dad, I had a dream."

We asked, "What's the dream?"

He then told us that while we were driving, he fell asleep; and in this dream, he saw a huge angelic being who lifted the car and pushed it forward. My parents asked him again whether he had experienced that, and he said yes. At that moment, we showed him the time of arrival. A journey that usually takes six to seven hours took 3.25 hours for us.

A similar incident took place when I was hosting a conference. One of the guest speakers, Tim Storey, had to catch his flight back to LA on Saturday morning, and we had to drop him off at 9:00 a.m. My armor-bearer and I had to open the sanctuary by 10:00 a.m. for service. We were talking about the supernatural move of God in our lives and around the world. We dropped Tim Storey off a few minutes past 9:00 a.m. My armor-bearer at that time was concerned about who would open the church by 10:00 a.m. I called my wife and others who had the keys to kindly go and open the door by 10:00 a.m. because there was no way we could have made it back there in time. We knew our arrival time at the church for the morning session would be 10:35 a.m. to 10:45 a.m.

As we drove off from the airport, we talked and did not pay attention to the road. At exactly 9:45 a.m., we were at the exit into Ashtabula. We were shocked, and he began to cry like a baby. It was like things went too fast before us. I was astonished. We both were shaking. We thanked God while my armor-bear cried with joy all day. My armor-bearer was so excited to have had such an experience. He had only heard about it, and now, he experienced it. Surprisingly, we were the first to arrive, so we opened the church and prepared for service. That morning, as we shared our experience with the church, the glory of God descended on the service.

This is precisely what happened when God sent His angels to release Peter from prison. God released His angel to set him free and go through fortified gates. Even in the story of Elijah, when he stood at the top of the mountain and prayed for rain, God quickly made provision. And thus, Elijah was translated from the top of the mountain. Elijah outran Ahab because of God's divine intervention. Similarly, God's assistance is always available to take us from point A to point B if we replace doubt and worry with faith and prayer.

God's Spiritual Deliverance

Psalm 91:1–3 (NKJV) is a typical passage from the Bible used as a prayer for protection. It says, "He who dwells in the secret place of the Most High shall abide under the shadow of the Almighty. I will say of the Lord, 'He is my refuge and my fortress; my God, in whom I trust.'" Psalm 91:11 (NKJV) says, "For He shall give His angels charge over you, To keep you in all your ways."

The word *charge* means "responsibility for." You've got angels watching over you. You are God's ambassador here on earth. Hebrews 12:22 (NKJV) says, "An immeasurable company of angels." These angels are on assignment for heaven and the earth. The Creator and the Master is, therefore, called the Lord of Hosts. He is the Lord of the Hosts of all the angels; He is the Lord of all. Lord means "owner." He owns them. They are under his authority and delegated power. They are the ones who carry out his desires. He is ultimately responsible for all angels.

This psalm continues with rich promises of supernatural provision and divine protection from God. It lists all God's blessings for us and proves how He has charged His angels to take care of us. Along with these blessings, we see God's own divine intervention and deliverance. Everything that happens is at the command of the Lord. God commands His angels to defeat evil forces. He opens the gates of heaven for blessings and favor and grants us long life. Since the beginning of the Bible, we have seen the presence of these angelic beings in the lives of the chosen people. For example, in the case of Lot, two angels visited him to save him and his household from the punishment that was going to be bestowed on Sodom. Just like this, we see angelic beings sent as messengers to various people such as Sarah, Abraham's wife; Moses; and many others, even in the New Testament. The purpose is to give direction and guidance and help them in times of difficulty.

In Acts 16: 25–29 (NKJV), we see a great miracle when Paul and Silas are seized because they cast out an evil spirit in the name of Jesus. It is written:

> But at midnight Paul and Silas were praying and singing hymns to God, and the prisoners were listening to them. Suddenly there was a great earthquake, so that the foundations of the prison were shaken; and immediately all the doors were opened and everyone's chains were loosed. And the keeper of the prison, awaking from sleep and seeing the prison doors open, supposing the prisoners had fled, drew his sword and was about to kill himself. But Paul called with a loud voice, saying, "Do yourself no harm, for we are all here." Then he called for a light, ran in, and fell down trembling before Paul and Silas. And he brought them out and said, "Sirs, what must I do to be saved?"

In the night, the Lord had sent His angels to break open the prison doors and unfasten their chains for them. Paul and Silas had not given in to fear and worry. Instead, they had prayed all night and sang hymns. Because God saw their faithfulness, He sent His angels to protect them. As a result, they were freed; and the people around them who also had faith, the jailer's family, were saved that night.

The destiny helpers were released at midnight for Paul and Silas, which shows how God is ready to send them for us even in the darkest hours of our lives. Therefore, we do not need to let worry occupy our hearts when God cares so much more for us.

When my son was a little younger, he would often wake up from sleep after 3:00 a.m. and cry uncontrollably. He would scream and jump out of his bed. This scenario went on for about a week. My wife and I decided to go and pray in the room. However, this did not help much, so I told my wife that I would sleep in his room with him.

The night I went to sleep in his room, God showed me in a dream a demonic being that stood at the foot of his bed. I prayed and bound that demon. Suddenly, I saw ropes tied around this demonic creature. After this demon was tied, I heard a voice that said, "Cast this demonic being into hell," and so I rebuked and cast it back to hell in the name of Jesus. In a quick flash, a light came into the room and pushed the demonic creature away. I believe it was a warrior angel released by God to cast this demon out of my son's room and back to where he belonged.

Once again, God had released his destiny helpers to intervene in our affairs on earth and release us from the bondage of demonic forces. God has given us a name that is above every name, and that name is Jesus. Why should you live in fear? We must call on the name.

Friends and family—these are people of your clan whom God uses to build you up and help you reach heights. They may be from your generation or someone very close to you. A biblical example of this is Aaron in the book of Exodus, who is the brother of Moses. Throughout Moses's years of leadership, Aaron stayed by his side and assisted him. He was also a godly man whom God chose for the vocation of priesthood for the Israelites. The Bible tells us that God provides these godly people to help us reach our destiny. These people play a massive part in helping us achieve it. Remember that before any favor is manifested in the physical, the breakthrough takes place in the spiritual realm. God will also bring people into your life in times of difficulties. God will make sure you feel supported and loved. A man of God and the congregants were building a big sanctuary in Calabar, Nigeria.

It got to a point where all funds were depleted, and they became a subject of laughter for the people. It became very difficult to accomplish the task. One day, the pastor was about to take a flight back home to Calabar. He purchased an economy ticket. When he got to the airport, he felt in his spirit strongly to upgrade to business class. This pastor was battling with this voice. *I need more to complete the church building. Why an upgrade?* The pastor finally surrendered to this voice and upgraded his ticket. He sat close to an individual in the business class. They got into a conversation, and he prayed for this individual. He asked for the pastor's business card, but the pastor did not give it to him. As soon as the door opened, this man stepped out; and to the surprise of this pastor, an entourage came to receive the man.

Immediately, the pastor ran down the stairs and reminded the man that he had asked for his credentials, and the pastor then gave the man his card. The man took the credentials and later called to visit the pastor's church. He came by and saw that the church was struggling. Upon leaving the premises, he turned to the pastor and said he would provide the funds to complete the church building. The pastor was surprised and overjoyed. Indeed, this individual fulfilled his pledge.

People, you don't need to worry! God has assigned an individual to come and meet that need. If God could connect Peter with Cornelius (Acts 10), what more of you? If you have done all that you can, let go and let God. Destiny helpers will connect you to the right people this season in Jesus's name. In Jeremiah 33:3 (NKJV), God tells us, "Call to Me, and I will answer you and show you great and mighty things, which you do not know."

There are supernatural blessings kept in the heavenly realms. They are accessible if we call to Him and claim those blessings for ourselves. God does not want us to mindlessly spend our lives on earth and then die without accomplishing anything. He wants us to succeed in the present life and the eternal life to follow. Therefore, we need to place our lives into His hands so that He can help us accomplish our purpose here on earth. We need to pray to Him and ask with faith that we may obtain His preordained blessings.

In the process of achieving this, you may find yourself all alone. You may have to deal with people who criticize you and undermine your abilities as you embark on this journey with God. The truth is that you are not alone. The Bible says in Romans 8:31 (NKJV), "What then shall we say to these things? If God is for us, who can be against us?" When God is by your side, everything will fall into its proper place. He will prepare a way for you and give you divine protection. There may be distractions from the evil one who will magnify your inabilities and weaknesses, and you begin to lose hope.

In such situations, the goal must be to keep your gaze fixed on Jesus Christ. You are exactly where you are supposed to be, and in due time, your breakthrough will arrive. The devil will try to place certain people in your life to hinder you from succeeding or accomplishing your purpose here on earth. Believe that the Holy Spirit and the host of angels are by your side. Until then, you must learn to surrender to the will of God. If you place your life in God's hands and submit to Him, then He will let everything happen for your good. God will bring situations or use people or even his divine protection to save and assist you.

We must embrace the destiny helpers that God has designed for us instead of choosing the path of sin. Sin may seem appealing for some time, but its path leads to destruction. The destiny that God has ordained is filled with success, protection, as well as provision.

> "God does not want us to mindlessly spend our lives on earth and then die without accomplishing anything."

Demonic principalities are probably the most dangerous ones to humans. These are also known as demonic angels assigned by Satan over nations or territories. Why? It indicates that these are demonic angels who are assigned to every nation, along with a hierarchy of lesser demonic angels under them. The Bible calls them principalities.

In Daniel 10:11–20 (NKJV), you remember that the prince of Persia withheld Daniel's answer to prayer. This demonic angel was fighting against the work of God and stopping the prayer of Daniel. Why are they called principalities? According to the *Merriam-Webster Dictionary*, they're called principalities because they are given the responsibilities of a principal over territory or jurisdiction. They are also called princes. A prince or principality influences laws and principles that control societies. It is very important to understand that.

Principalities, in theology, are referred to as an order of angels with powers often in conflict with God. They influence laws that create principles by which people live. They deal with precepts; in other words, they get into the educational system and put principles in books through people they influence to believe certain precepts. An entire generation of children is then taught to think a certain way. Demons love to control the mountain of education and introduce all ungodly principles. Ungodly principles could be systems of belief or behaviors that are contrary to the ways of God, causing children to dishonor and disobey Him.

The next area demons love to control is the media: television, radio, and music. Today's PG or PG-13 movies often have adult content with cursing and immorality. We no longer have a great kids' program because witchcraft and mermaid spirits have invaded the media. What you watch opens either a heavenly portal or a demonic portal in your home. What you watch or focus on will cause activation in the spirit and will manifest in the physical. That is how most of the demonic spirits of worry, frustration, depression, fear, and isolation get into the lives of individuals. How about adultery and fornication? The more you watch TV programs full of adultery, fornication, and perversion, the more seeds are sown in your soul. Eventually, you no longer even notice or consider them to be negative influences. Every week, a demonic principle is coming through your mind. Now, a principle is a what? A law by which you live. How did the law come into your mind? Through the visual and audio mechanisms of television.

The Bible says your thoughts become a stronghold. The Bible says in Ephesians 6, we fight not against flesh and blood but against principalities and powers and wicked spirits in high places, therefore casting down imaginations and every high thing that exalts itself against the knowledge of God and bringing into captivity every thought. In other words, you better watch what you are watching and listen to the music you are listening to because the devil is at work defining and creating patterns of thought.

Wrestling

When I was single, I was a huge fan of WWE. I would watch all the pay-per-view matches. The anticipation of looking forward to Mondays and Fridays or events was high. It took much of my time. Whenever I watched a match, I noticed that the atmosphere in my home would change. After the match, I would spend days trying to create the right atmosphere in my home. To pray or study the Bible was a struggle. I would try to pray, but the atmosphere would be almost suffocating. Sometimes, after I watched the scantily clad ladies on the show, the demonic spirit of masturbation would invade my life; it became a struggle. I wept before God, yet I would tune in to watch for three to four hours of these events. I could spend three hours watching WWE, but I would rarely spend that amount of time in the presence of God to build an intimate relationship with Him.

I went for about two weeks without watching any WWE matches to rededicate myself to the Holy Spirit; the atmosphere was so great in my home during that time. I will never forget this particular day I came home from work. For some reason, I had the TV on, and a WWE main event was on. Immediately, the Holy Spirit opened my eyes, and I saw the most frightening thing happen. The atmosphere in my home changed with a strong demonic smell. An ungodly creature had come into my home. I screamed, turned off the TV, and began to pray. Immediately, that demonic atmosphere left my home, and the atmosphere of heaven invaded my living room. On this day, the Holy Spirit made me understand that whenever I watched such programs, the heavenly realm gave way to the demonic realm. What you spend your time watching or listening to will either welcome Jesus Christ into your life and home or welcome Satan and his demons.

While in Bible school, we were told of a Christian boy who locked himself in the room studying while listening to ungodly heavy metal or rock music. Later, the demonic spirits possessed him, and he began to shout in the room. It was so intense that they had to break the door to get to him. The parents found out that he was cutting himself while shouting to the music. The pastors were called immediately, and that demonic spirit was cast out!

Some people are unaware that they are being controlled by Satan. Colossians 2:15 (AMP) says, "When He had disarmed the rulers and authorities [those supernatural forces of evil operating against us], He made a public example of them [exhibiting them as captives in His triumphal procession], having triumphed over them through the cross."

Ephesians (NLT) 3:10 says, "God's purpose in all this was to use the church to display his wisdom in its rich variety to all the unseen rulers and authorities in the heavenly places." He tells us that God intends for all the spirits, demons, and everyone else to see His wisdom through the church. To overcome worry, we need to embrace God's principles, which produce blessings.

That is why we need to pray and intercede. Over us in the air are demonic powers under the control of principalities, whose job is to create precepts for the whole nation to live by against the ways of God.

When a nation yields to a demonic principle, it becomes law and a constitutional sin. In other words, it creates a kind of compromise with sin and promotes ungodly practices. When a nation accepts such acts, it draws God's judgment.

For individuals living in sin, their fate will include suffering because of their bad choices, and their spirit will end up in hell for all eternity. For this, the Lord cannot be blamed because they choose the course of their lives for themselves.

Romans 1:24–26 (NKJV) explains this: "Therefore God also gave them up to uncleanness, in the lusts of their hearts, to dishonor their bodies among themselves who exchanged the truth of God for the lie, and worshiped and served the creature rather than the Creator, who is blessed forever. Amen. For this reason, God gave them up to vile passions. For even their women exchanged the natural use for what is against nature."

God leaves the sinful people on their own after their persistent denial of the love and grace of God. He stops providing his guidance, protection, and blessings to them. They are left to bear the result of their wrong decisions. On the other hand, the godly still have access to His protection and favor. These blessings remain with them until they finally enter heaven to stay with the Lord forever. Therefore, we are predestined to live a life of success. We are made to accomplish great things to bring glory to His name. God has deposited unique sets of skills and talents in each of us, and He wants us to utilize them to the fullest. All we need to do is recognize them and put them to productive use in their due time. We need to embrace His will, and His Spirit will guide us to the purpose and destiny that He has prepared.

God does not want to see any of us fail. He wants us to seek Him in times of hardships so He can pull us out of our difficulties. But the mistake that most of us make is going astray from Him in moments of dire need. We fall away immediately and forget all His promises. We allow worry and fear to rule over us, which slowly takes us to the path of negativity and sin. We are born to stand for righteousness, purity, holiness, and holiness in marriage between a man and a woman.

There are demonic powers all over this country, working in your school, in your colleges, and on your job. They run the business downtown and work in education, and you must deal with them using prayer. The Bible says, "The weapons of our warfare are not carnal, but they are spiritual, and they are mighty through God to the pulling down of strongholds." We must be in continuous fasting and prayer. You can't win without prayer; you can't even go in and out of your house without praying. These demons are everywhere, and they are working against you. They're working with principalities and powers, and you must fight them using prayer. Their purpose is to make sure you do not have a relationship with God and fill your heart with the cares of life, which produces worry and fear. You're fighting against spirits.

Ambassadors of Heaven

"Now then, we are ambassadors for Christ, as though God were pleading through us: we implore you on Christ's behalf, be reconciled to God" (2 Corinthians 5:20 NKJV).

I am an ambassador of God. I am the representative of heaven here on earth. An ambassador is the representative of the nation. For example, the U.S. ambassador to Malaysia represents the president of the United States. He speaks on behalf of the president of the United States. He knows who he is. He doesn't live in fear. If anybody wanted to touch him, they were in trouble. The entire nation of the United States will come against a nation that touches its ambassador. And the ambassador representing that nation in a foreign country has an entourage. He doesn't go anywhere alone. An ambassador doesn't live a broke life. Oh, we are getting somewhere. They don't have the mentality of a broke life. Are you getting the picture?

You and I are ambassadors of heaven. We represent heaven here on earth. Destiny helpers are at our disposal in times of need; we are never alone. I know of a great man of God, the late archbishop Benson Idahosa. My parents were close to him and remain close to his wife, Archbishop Margaret Idahosa. She visited us in Maryland and told us this great testimony of her late husband.

Late Archbishop Benson Idahosa's Testimony

Some months after the archbishop's dedication of The Faith Arena—then the largest church auditorium in the whole of Africa at Upper Adesuwa, GRA, Benin—the news went around Nigeria that witches from all over the globe had met in Chicago, Illinois (USA), and they decided to hold their first international conference in Nigeria. The venue was identified as Benin City. The chief host of the witches' meeting, an academician of Bini origin, held a press conference and informed the Nigerian Television Authority (NTA) Benin and newspapers, such as the *Tribune*, *Sketch*, and *Punch*, that this first world conference hosting witches and wizards would be held in Benin. Archbishop Idahosa was informed; and true to himself, in the next edition of *Idahosa and You*, a program of the Idahosa World Outreach, he said it could not be accurate as it was impossible.

The church in Nigeria heard that the witches were holding a conference and were troubled. They rallied everybody to cry out to God. The late archbishop Benson Idahosa said, "Why are you all gathering to cry to God?" The press met Idahosa and asked what exactly was not possible and what the consequences were, if any? "Witches from the world could not come to Benin," insisted Benson as he would "kill them all." The city became abuzz.

The press characteristically returned to the chief host to inform him about Idahosa's response. He boasted, "Not even

God can stop it! I am a wizard, and I know the power we carry." The next day, all the headlines of the national dailies carried the story on their front pages. Idahosa was informed about the response of the chief wizard host that God could not stop the event from being held. "Yes, he is correct," said Archbishop Idahosa. "That is why I am here. God does not need to waste his time considering matters as trivial as stopping the conference of witches."

Idahosa sought to know how many witches were expected in Benin. "About 9,800 of them," he was told. The press visited his house to advise him against the risk he was taking by challenging witches openly. "Witches are not to be toiled with. Be careful. Do not throw your life away. It is not compulsory to take up these challenges. You are already known by the power of God manifesting in your life. You don't have any point to prove," they said.

Idahosa responded, "Those who take care do not take charge, and those who take charge do not take care."

The chief host had also warned that Idahosa was a busybody, merely risking his life. When Idahosa insisted that there would be no witches' conference in Benin, the media asked if he was ready to tell the whole nation. They told him they intended to arrange a TV program for the chief wizard to meet face-to-face to defend their positions. He replied in the affirmative. Idahosa loved open confrontations.

About a week later, they were both on-air. The moderator started by saying, "Gentlemen, we don't want anybody to get hurt." He then asked Idahosa's disputant, "Chief Host, are you really sure you are bringing 9,800 witches from all over the world?" The moderator got a resounding yes. The moderator then faced Idahosa, "Dr. Idahosa, are you sure you are going to be able to stop this conference of wizards and witches?"

"It is not that I am *going to* stop it. I have stopped it," replied the archbishop, now raising his voice.

The moderator then told them both, "Are you really ready? I am now going to grant you time to tell us how serious your position is and how strong the power of your God is." He beckoned on Idahosa and the chief host; both said they were ready. Quickly chiming in, Idahosa requested to pray before the program ended, as he intended to kill the wizard through prayers on live TV. Reluctantly, the moderator accepted. The chief host was unshaken.

The wizard spoke first for about 27 minutes, quoting copiously from the Old Testament of the Bible, Egyptian hieroglyphics, British writings, Jewish scrolls, Indian Maharaja, and other mystical books. As he ended, the moderator asked if Idahosa had heard the chief wizard. He said he had. "What do you have to say?" Idahosa was asked.

"There is nothing to say. I said the proposed conference is canceled."

"How?" the moderator asked.

The archbishop then opened the Bible and quickly read passages from Exodus, Leviticus, Deuteronomy, and some New Testament verses. He asked how many minutes he had left and was told, "Just five."

"Fine, it is time for somebody to report to his Maker!" he exclaimed, rising from his seat. There was pandemonium in the studio. With everyone watching, he turned to the self-proclaimed wizard and chief host and asked, "I just need an answer from you. Your life is hanging on your answer. A witch is not supposed to live, and I intend to kill you now if you are one." At home and in the studio, viewers were glued to their screens. The tension was palpable all around. "Now answer me and this large viewing audience in one or two words. Are you a wizard? Just answer yes or no."

"I am not."

"What did you say? Because I am ready to pray," Idahosa prompted.

"I am not a wizard," the frightened man replied.

"Then there is no need to go on. Stand up and leave the studio!"

The chief host quickly walked out as sighs of relief filled the studio. The Christians among the TV crew smiled and kept giving one another the thumbs-up sign. Benson Idahosa began to fire off in tongues.

The following day, the chief host visited the archbishop's office and even collected a Bible. However, he still insisted to the media that the conference would be held in seven days. The media contacted Idahosa to inform him. "Is the conference still holding or not?"

"No comment," Benson Idahosa responded, "but if the conference still holds, I will burn my Bible. I say it is canceled."

On the day of the opening, there was no conference. The next day, Archbishop Idahosa traveled to Lagos to see General Ibrahim Badamasi Babangida, a Muslim. "As you are very well aware, I told the whole nation that the conference of the witches would not be held in this country, and you can see that it did not take place."

"Yes," replied the president. "When I saw you and that fellow defending your beliefs and positions, I sent a telex to all our embassies not to allow even one witch or wizard into Nigeria. They were all denied visas."

Why would Idahosa be so bold? Because he knew who he was, an ambassador of heaven here on earth. And when he, Benson Idahosa, speaks, things must happen. And he spoke and declared, and the witches never met. You see, we are living in an era where we need to resist worries because we know who we are in Christ. God has given you power. Everything you need has been deposited in you. You've just got to speak! "Devil, get out of my house! Devil, get out of my body! Sickness, depart!" You've just got to speak because the words that come out of your mouth carry power. You have an entourage of heaven around you. The angels of heaven walk with you. When you speak, they go immediately and put your words to work. You've got to know who you are. Your words will render every principality powerless if you believe in Jesus Christ. Psalm 34:7 (NKJV) says, "The angel of the LORD encamps around those who fear him, and he delivers them."

Manifesting the Glory of God: My Journey from Indiana to Atlanta

I was flying from Indiana to Atlanta. When I arrived at the airport, the ticket they gave me was a standby ticket. Oh, I don't like standby tickets because you don't know when you're going to fly. I waited, and the first plane left, then the second plane. Only one remaining flight would get me to Atlanta on time for the service that night at seven. It was 4:00 p.m., and I was still at the airport. I went to this lady at the airline's counter and explained that I needed to get on this flight.

"I have a meeting tonight, and I am going to be on this flight."

She said, "Well, the flight is full."

I said, "I respect your opinion that the flight is full, but I have a meeting tonight and have to be on this flight to Atlanta."

109

She said, "The flight is full."

I sat down and spoke to the Lord. I said, "Lord, I need to catch this flight. People are waiting to be ministered to. People are waiting to experience miracles from You this evening. Lord, I pray in Your precious name to release Your angel to get me on that flight and have a seat available for me." All the passengers boarded the flight. I was sitting alone and began to praise God within me.

I prayed to God from a place of trust and not worry. As I sat there, the phone to the airline's counter rang. When the airline representative put the phone down, she turned and looked at me. She said, "You know what, there's something different about you."

I said, "It is the favor of God."

She told me to come to the counter. "OK, let me tell you what's happening." She said, "A lady on the plane became uncomfortable with the seat that she was given and wanted to get off the flight so she could arrange to fly the following day. She's uncomfortable sitting in that particular window seat." Just then, they opened the door, and she walked out.

I began to laugh and said, "Thank you, Lord. Thank you, Lord. Thank you, Lord." I went and sat on the plane, and by the grace of God, I made it to the service. The Lord did wonderful miracles; we just need to know who we are in Him.

The Pagan Priest Repents

The story is based on the book *Like a Mighty Wind* by Mel Tari. Mel Tari, a personal friend of mine and renowned evangelist God used in the early years of Indonesia's revival, remembers how one of the teams went to a village to preach the gospel. The pagan priest said to them, "You can preach to us about Jesus, but we want to tell you we have known the devil for many generations. If we want healing, the devil gives it. If we want rain, the devil gives that. Whatever we want, the devil supplies. We have our own Bible too. Our gods supply all our needs according to their riches."

Of course, they didn't have a real Bible like ours. But they had recorded many unusual experiences and evil manifestations, and they worshipped these. "If you tell us about the new God, let Him prove that He is more powerful than our gods," the priest told the team.

The team didn't know what to do, so they prayed together and asked the Lord for help. The Lord said, "Tell them if they want your God to prove Himself to them that He is more powerful than their gods or demons, let them gather together, and I will prove myself."

The team said to the head pagan priest, "Gather all your people and tell them to come, and we will see what will happen." The pagan priest was excited. He wanted to see if the Christian God could prove himself. They came together, about one thousand of them, with the head pagan priest in the front. The team stood across from them.

The team members lifted their hands and said, "God, You said for us to go out and preach the gospel and that many signs shall follow those who believe, that in Your name, they shall cast out devils. God, these people want You to prove Yourself that You are more powerful than their devils. Now, in the name of Jesus, we bind and cast out all demonic power that has ruled these villages and people for many generations. Because of Christ's shed blood on Calvary, we command them to leave in the name of Jesus." After this simple prayer, they just said amen, looked at one another, and let God do the rest.

Soon, the head pagan priest began to tremble. He began to cry and said, "Brothers, sirs, I want your God, Jesus, right now." It was such a quick transformation; the team members didn't know what to say.

"Why did you change your mind, sir?" one of them finally asked.

"Oh, Jesus is more powerful than the devils," he replied.

"How do you know that?" one of the team members asked.

"I am a pagan priest," he replied. "I have talked with the devils. I know many of them by name." Then he started to cry and couldn't control himself.

"What is the matter? We don't know what is going on," someone on the team said.

"Yes, yes, I know," the pagan priest replied. "But when you prayed in the name of Jesus and bound all the demonic power here and commanded them to flee, do you know what happened?"

"No," the team said. "We don't know what happened. Just tell us what happened."

"I'll tell you," said the priest. "I saw with my own eyes and heard with my own ears all the demonic power that has ruled this village. They just gathered, one by one, from the biggest to the smallest, and they ran away, crying, 'Jesus won't permit us to stay here. We must go because Jesus wants these people.' Jesus must be a tremendous God. I want to know Jesus."

The team just said simply, "If you want Jesus, we want to show you the way." They opened the Bible and simply showed him how to accept Jesus Christ as his own personal Savior. He did it right away, and the other people did it right afterward. Praise God!

Cherubim in the End-Times

Genesis 3:24 (NKJV) says, "So He drove out the man; and He placed cherubim at the east of the garden of Eden, and a flaming sword which turned every way, to guard the way to the tree of life."

Another group of God's angels is called cherubim. A cherubim is a high-ranking angel connected with God's retributive and redemptive purposes. Every time you see a cherub, it has to do with redemption or retribution. Whenever you see the word *cherubim*, you see God. They are very protective angels. Cherubim are described as serving God's will and performing divine duties in the earthly realm. These are powerful heavenly beings with four faces and four wings.

My Encounter

One day, around 4:00 p.m., I was in my prayer room. As I began to pray, my eyes were closed. Suddenly, I saw the sky open, and I saw some giant wings. I had never seen anything like it in my life. The noise that accompanied these beings breaking through the sky was one I never heard before. It happened in a flash, and I could not see the rest. Immediately, the room I was in literally shook. I was scared because of the shaking. I asked the Lord, "What just happened? What did I see?"

I heard His voice like the sound of many rivers and other sounds I can't explain, "I have released a cherub over the ministry I have called you to operate in."

I was perplexed. With much grace, I asked Him a question, "How will they believe me if I said cherubs are ready to be released more into our realm for this end-time glorious harvest?"

The Lord spoke to me and said, "Remember what happened in Genesis 3? When I drove man from the Garden of Eden, a cherub was released to close that realm and protect it. So are the cherubs being released at this hour to protect the glory being released here on earth upon every true born-again believer."

That might not make sense to you, but the Bible says God will pour out His spirit on all flesh so the greatest manifestation of God's power here on earth shall be seen. Creative miracles, signs, and wonders will be the norm. Many will come to Jesus.

The Bible warns us to watch out for false teachers and look at their fruits. Because of hunger, fame, and riches, some have consulted the demonic realm for powers. Jesus told me that the church should not worry or be concerned with false teachers, pastors, prophets, etc. Jesus said, "Son, do you remember the story of Moses and Pharaoh?" Remember, Moses showed up to Pharaoh with his staff. He placed the staff on the ground, and it turned into a snake. Pharaoh also called his magicians, who displayed the same thing. On both sides, the staff turned into a snake, but there was a clear difference at the end. The genuine, anointed staff of Moses swallowed that of the magicians," Jesus said. "That's exactly what's going to happen in these end-times. The glory of God will be so strong that even the counterfeits won't be able to stand."

That's why we, as the body of Christ, need to be in the presence of Jesus Christ constantly. You are a candidate for the Holy Spirit to use. This end-time glory movement is not just for pastors, apostles, etc., but for everyone who makes his or herself available to God. We are vessels, and He is willing to pour into us. When His destiny helpers are released to accompany and protect us, you don't need to worry that God has your back as an individual and as a ministry.

"And there I will meet with you, and I will speak with you from above the mercy seat, from between the two cherubim which are on the ark of the Testimony, about everything which

114

I will give you in commandment to the children of Israel" (Exodus 25:22 NKJV).

Cherubim are the angels chosen to watch over the mercy seat because they protect God's presence; they are violently protective of God's holiness. The presence of God around us also needs to be protected. Cherubim are described as having the face of a lion, a man's face, the face of an ox, and the face of an eagle. A godly character opens up the realm of heaven over your life, home, and ministry. Whenever we say "In the name of Jesus," we are simply saying in the character of Jesus. That name carries the power to demolish every demonic spirit and principality. For it to be effective in our lives, we must put on the character of Jesus Christ. A lion represents strength. A man's face represents intelligence. The ox represents service and obedience, while the face of the eagle represents sharp sight and focus.

Angels are intelligent with the ability to make decisions. With such an angelic presence around you, you can see clearly what God sees about you. They watch the presence of the Lord for any contamination. In other words, when the Bible says if you touch God's holiness, you will die, it means these angels kill. Remember Ananias and Sapphira in Acts 5? They lied in the presence of God's servant, and they both died. God doesn't kill; it's the cherubim that get the job done. The flaming sword they carry constantly guards the presence of the Lord. When you come into God's presence contaminated, they could wipe you out. The flame of the sword is reflective of their power to destroy. Therefore, the cherubim are very extraordinary creatures built to defend and protect the holiness of God.

The cherubim are committed entirely to serving God and are always obedient to Him. They always do His bidding. They are entrusted with the holiness of God. Imagine such power being released to move with you in the end-times. You will automatically yield yourself to be used by God and serve in every capacity to the glory of God.

Lastly, a team accompanied my wife and me to Nicaragua for a crusade. The attendance was great, about one thousand plus in the hall. The atmosphere on the first day was too tight. No miracles. Nothing happened. I spoke to the team, and we prayed. I went to bed and had a dream. I was driving on a beautiful road in this dream when I saw a gentleman standing and waving for me to stop. A thought came to me, asking, *Why should I stop for a stranger? I don't know him.* Yet within me, there was an urge to stop. I did stop, and this gentleman asked if he could ride my car. I agreed; and immediately, when he stepped foot into the car, the entire atmosphere changed. I tried to see His face, but I couldn't. The atmosphere was so sweet.

As we drove, we talked, and he was giving me powerful advice. While in the car, I knew the car was moving, but I was not in control. He then said, 'Thank you for inviting me. Always make it a priority to invite me." When he said that, I woke up and shared it with my wife, then the group. We welcomed the Holy Spirit with His entourage into the meeting. We knew that God was going to move awesomely that night because of the encounter.

When we arrived at the meeting place, the Lord opened my eyes, and I saw a being engulfed in a flame of many colors at the back of the church. I immediately told the people while onstage that the angel of the Lord carrying His fire had arrived. The Holy Spirit then instructed me to let the people worship the Lord. As soon as we started worshipping Jesus Christ, the people from the back came to the front, and the choir began to fall under the power of God with no hands placed on them. Deliverance and miracles began to take place across the hall. Deaf ears were opened, legs that were shorter grew to match the other, and one person walked away without the wheelchair. People gave their lives to Jesus while others rededicated themselves, and the young people were on fire for God. Wherever we have gone, we see this angel carrying the fire of God. Passion for God is being birthed or rebirthed for the glory of God. Most of the time, we will see the liquid fire of God over people.

I believe that these are the angels that serve under the seraphim mentioned in Isaiah 6:2. They are seen as the highest order of angels. The name *seraphim* means "burning one." Seraphim have six wings. They are right in the fire of God and were used to put coal on the prophet's tongue. They come directly from the altar of God and are engulfed in the fire of God.

Isaiah 6:6–7 (NKJV) says, "Then one of the seraphim flew to me, having in his hand a live coal which he had taken with the tongs from the altar. And he touched my mouth with it and said: 'Behold, this has touched your lips; Your iniquity is taken away, And your sin purged.'"

Angels are living proof that there's much about the world we don't understand. We can't see them; they are invisible unless they reveal themselves. It also proves to us that we see life through a glass dimly. Life is much bigger than what you see. However, there are things that we can learn from the angels of God.

Here Are Some Important Truths

Angels were created to serve God and His children. They are not made to be worshipped; they are servants. "Are they not all ministering spirits sent forth to minister for those who will inherit salvation" (Hebrews 1:14 NKJV).

Angels dispense God's justice and judgment. Look at Numbers 22:20–33. In verse 22 (NKJV), it is recorded, "And

God's anger was kindled because he went: and the angel of the LORD stood in the way for an adversary against him ... And the ass saw me, and turned from me these three times: unless she had turned from me, surely now also I had slain thee, and saved her alive."

No matter how much God loves you and cares for you, you must obey God. You don't get away with anything with God. God is faithful to his word. Today, you and I rejoice over the protection and the care of angels. We thank God for that powerful servant who is assigned to comfort us and watch over us. But suppose we do not heed the invitation to become heirs of God (accepting Jesus Christ) so that they can serve us. In that case, we too will suffer damnation just like the devil and his angels.

Angels remind us then of two choices. We can live with the ones in heaven, or we can live with the ones in hell. No matter where you go, you will encounter angels. The choice today is up to you. If you don't know Christ as your Lord and Savior, there is no way to live with God's angels and the glory of the heavenly hosts. If you do know Him, there's a guarantee that you will be with them. But if you don't know Jesus, you can ask Him to come into your heart right now. Ask Jesus to forgive you of all your sins and be the Lord of your life.

8

⤜⬥⬥⬥⥟

Battlefield Mind

For as he thinks in his heart, so is he.

—Proverbs 23:7 (NKJV)

What you dwell on, think on, and meditate on is what you will become. Do you realize your thoughts are so powerful that they draw things to you? Thinking is where it starts, not speaking. In Proverbs 30:32 (NKJV), the writer Solomon says, "If you have been foolish in exalting yourself, Or if you have devised evil, put your hand on your mouth!"

Satan is after your thoughts, but so is God. What you think about continuously, you become. You must watch your thoughts and what you say. Have you ever asked the question, why did the devil torment Job with loss and sickness? Let's look at Job 1:8–12 (NKJV) in the Bible. Here, we recognize that Satan visited God after walking to and fro on earth:

> Then the Lord said to Satan, "Have you considered My servant Job, that *there is* none like him on the earth, a blameless and upright man, one who fears God and shuns evil?" So Satan answered the Lord and said, "Does Job fear God

for nothing? Have You not made a hedge around him, around his household, and around all that he has on every side? You have blessed the work of his hands, and his possessions have increased in the land. But now, stretch out Your hand and touch all that he has, and he will surely curse You to Your face!" And the Lord said to Satan, "Behold, all that he has *is* in your power; only do not lay a hand on his *person*."

God told Satan "All Job had was in his power" but not because of Job's sinfulness or God's anger. What Job had thought became a test to him. The story of Job is a prominent example in the Bible that gives us a clear picture of how far the devil can go to afflict people. The book of Job narrates how a man of God is made to suffer miserably for months at a time. He lost his seven sons, three daughters, and wealth in one day. He had open sores all over his body and was despised and rejected by his loved ones. We see his wife loathing him and his friends rebuking him. Imagine the depth of his suffering! Job suffered the emotional and mental pain of the loss of his children and went through the excruciating pain of physical ailments. He had painful sores on his body that he scraped with a broken piece of pottery.

When his friends visited him, he was in such bad condition that Job responded,

> When they came near enough to see Job, they could hardly recognize him. And in their great sorrow, they tore their clothes, then sprinkled dust on their heads and cried bitterly. For seven days and nights, they sat silently on the ground beside him, because they realized what terrible pain, he was in. (Job 2:12–13 NKJV)

Job was not an evildoer but rather a faithful and righteous man of God. He had always lived a holy life, revering God and refusing to do evil. He was blessed with abundance and God's favor, yet he was a humble person. These attributes were consistent, even through the darkest time of his life. I firmly believe that the cause of Job's trouble began with a thought that brought fear into his life. This fear or worry gave Satan access to torment Job.

Read the words of Job: "For the thing I greatly feared has come upon me, and what I dreaded has happened to me" (Job 3:25 NKJV).

Despite all the blessings in Job's life, there was this fear of losing it all. This caused Job to work not from a place of rest but in fear of loss. Those thoughts drew the situation he feared to him. What do you fear? I have encountered many who were sick because of fear.

The Bible makes it very clear in 2 Timothy 1:7 (NKJV): "For God has not given us a spirit of fear, but of power and of love and of a sound mind."

For Job to experience victory, he had to change his thought process by looking unto God and believing Him for a breakthrough.

Now, we also see that even though Satan was afflicting Job, nothing was beyond the will of God. He had permitted the devil to come into His servant's life. Through this, we learn two things. First, godly men can also be pressed from every side, facing the same challenges as others. Second, Satan does not have the power to kill us and cross the boundaries that have been set for him.

As we glance at the incident of the first sin, we see that our weaknesses and physical afflictions are inevitable because of our spiritual detachment from the presence of God. As Adam and Eve disobeyed the Lord, they were banished from the presence of God; and along with that, the gift of immortality was also taken away. While previously they possessed the perfection of God, they now became prone to the consequences of sin, which weakened their physical health and exposed them to further attacks of the devil. In the Garden of Eden, the enemy came with a thought and suggestion. Realize that today, demons will tell you, "You don't have this. You can't do that." Notice when he told Eve that God was holding something back. This wasn't even true! You're not missing anything. When you were created, God had everything set for you. Everything that you were going to do, He put in you.

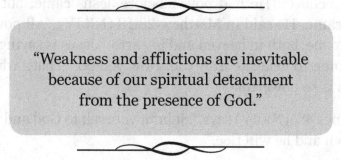

"Weakness and afflictions are inevitable because of our spiritual detachment from the presence of God."

It's all in your thinking. People are not poor because they have no money or can't find a good-paying job. They are poor because of the way they think. Are you following what I'm saying? In 1 Chronicles 4, Jabez found out his problem was not money. He didn't ask God for money. He asked God to enlarge his territory and his ability to receive in the way God sees him. You can receive what God has for you because your image has a lot to do with what you can do for God.

If you can get your thinking right, you can get your speaking right; and it will affect your spirit, which will relay it to your body for manifestation. In John 6:63 (NKJV), Jesus said, "My words, they are spirit, and they are life." Your thoughts and words will put either God's angels or Satan's demonic agents to work in your life. Spiritual things control natural things. God made you royalty. He made you speak, so when you speak, there should be an expectation that something will come to pass. Thinking is the primary issue!

"Finally, brethren, whatever things are true, whatever things are noble, whatever things are just, whatever things are pure, whatever things are lovely, whatever things are of good report, if there is any virtue and if there is anything praiseworthy— meditate on these things" (Philippians 4:8 NKJV).

The writer is saying, "Manage your mind." And then he tells us to "think on whatsoever things are true." Satan has no power over a believer. He had power before Jesus came, but once Jesus came, He said in Matthew 28:18 (NKJV), "All power is given to me, both in heaven and in earth." Jesus is saying now, "I'm going to delegate it to you. Now you go." That's why the church is so powerful.

James 4:7 (NKJV) says, "Submit yourself to God and resist the devil and he will flee."

God said, "You resist him, and he will flee." You've got to *resist* sickness. You must *resist* the temptation to say something mean. I can't get the devil to flee if I'm holding unforgiveness. It doesn't work. To overcome sickness, I must learn to yield to the Spirit of God. Therefore, we can see diseases that are so common today are mostly a consequence of the sins of humankind and their spiritual detachment from God.

Today, the devil uses various tactics to lead us astray from God. There are many external forces always luring us to sin to get us to lose our faith in God. Among these, physical affliction is one common strategy of the devil that he uses to torment us. As he has little power to cause direct harm to our spiritual state, he uses these forms of temptations to weaken us physically so that we may begin worrying and doubting God. He inflicts pain, and because of our human weaknesses, we give in to his schemes.

While illnesses are primarily associated with the physical state, the truth is that they can enter our lives in many ways. Ailments can be mental and emotional, but they all stem from the evil one attacking our faith in God.

In overcoming the spirit of worry, which might cause fear, you can speak life or death. Our words are not just sounds. We think our words are just noise, but they are not—they're spirit. Your spirit is a bag that holds words, and whatever words are in there when you come under attack, that's what comes out. Demons are waiting on your mouth to speak. They are perched, waiting for your conversation. Their job is to get you to loosen your tongue to say something that God didn't say. If you can fix your confession to be in line with the Word of God, all your physical, spiritual, and financial needs can and will be met.

While we know that sicknesses are part of the devil's vocation to bring us into temptation and try to weaken our faith, what are we supposed to do? Does it become inescapable for us? Is there a way out of the afflictions of life? While the world may give us many remedies and cures for suffering, the Bible gives us only one treatment: the blood of Jesus.

First Peter 2:24 (NKJV) states, "Who Himself bore our sins in His own body on the tree, that we, having died to sins, might live for righteousness—by whose stripes you were healed." Moreover, Isaiah 53:4–5 (NKJV) states, "Surely, He has borne our griefs and carried our sorrows; Yet we esteemed Him stricken, smitten by God, and afflicted. But He was wounded for our transgressions; He was bruised for our iniquities; The chastisement for our peace was upon Him, and by His stripes, we are healed."

The Bible tells us that the only thing that can completely heal us is believing in Jesus's saving act of redemption. The Bible tells us that physical, emotional, and mental suffering results from a grave spiritual shortcoming. This deficiency can only be overcome when we acknowledge Jesus as a personal savior and believe in the Word of God. When Jesus died on the cross, He did not just take up our sins but all the physical, mental, and emotional pain that human beings are bound to suffer. He bore it all on our behalf so that through Him, we could enjoy a life of blessings and joy.

As we glance at the incident of the first sin, we see that our weaknesses and physical afflictions are inevitable because of our spiritual detachment from the presence of God.

"By faith we understand that the worlds were framed by the Word of God, so that the things which are seen were not made of things which are visible" (Hebrews 11:3 NKJV).

It says in the scripture that everything that was made was made of things that are not visible. It does not say that God created everything out of nothing. Everything started from a single thought. Then God released His Spirit on earth. Genesis 1 says, "In the beginning, God created the heaven and the earth. The earth was without form and void, and darkness was on the face of the deep. And the Spirit of God was hovering over the face of the waters."

The first thing we see here is that God's own Spirit was released to move over the void and dark world. Regardless of the chaos or sickness in your body or life, the Holy Spirit is still hovering over you, waiting for one thing to take place.

Let's go back to Genesis 1. The next thing that took place was sound or word: "And God said, let there be light: and there was light" (Genesis 1:3 NKJV).

After the atmosphere of the glory and presence of God was on the earth, by the Holy Spirit, all God had to do was speak His Word amid chaos here on earth. When the Word was spoken, the Holy Spirit brought into existence what was invisible. In all our meetings, we saturate the atmosphere with worship. As His glory fills the room, then we speak His Word, and the Holy Spirit makes available the creative miracles for His People. The unseen or invisible things that God used to create are His presence and sound waves. Every creative miracle you need is available in the invisible realm. Even God was never recorded as opening His mouth to speak anything without the Holy Spirit first hovering, creating an atmosphere conducive to creative miracles.

In Genesis 2, God took the smallest particle or dust and mixed it with the highest DNA to create man. Every other thing, God commanded it to be. When it came to man, He physically formed man after His likeness. We are created in the image of God. God created us as physical beings. He breathed life into Adam, giving Adam the capacity to understand and communicate with God in the dimension of the spirit. John 4:24 (NKJV) states, "God is spirit." In Genesis 2:17 (NKJV), God told Adam that "but [only] from the tree of the knowledge [recognition] of good and evil you shall not eat, otherwise on the day that you eat from it, you shall most certainly die [because of your disobedience]." Adam disobeyed God, yet he lived. Adam did not die physically but spiritually. The Holy Spirit regenerates a person when he accepts Christ. In other words, we are reactivated spiritually.

As Christians, we must be aware of the spiritual reality of our words or confessions and familiarize ourselves with the high dimension of the Holy Spirit. The Holy Spirit is responsible for making the invisible visible. We are living in the age of the Holy Spirit. To be successful, we must not only recognize His work but also develop a personal relationship with the Holy

Spirit and learn to know Him. The Holy Spirit is a person and can be grieved (see Ephesians 4:30–32).

Interestingly, He is the source of God's dynamic power. Though He can form the earth and move mountains, He can be limited by a Christian's disobedience. He is the spirit of truth. He is called the spirit of wisdom, understanding, knowledge, and judgment.

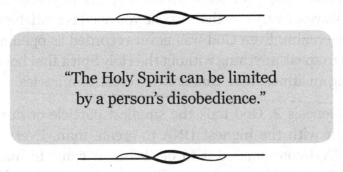

"The Holy Spirit can be limited
by a person's disobedicnce."

The Holy Spirit operates in three levels of relationship with man. Jesus said He would be *with* us, *in* us, and *upon* us.

The Holy Spirit Is *with* Us

He is with us to bring conviction of sin (John 16:8–11). The Holy Spirit is the wind of God. The metaphor of wind is used to describe the Holy Spirit because the wind is felt and not seen. Wind can be powerful or gentle and is experienced everywhere in the world at the same time. By sending the Holy Spirit, Jesus could break the limitations of being in one place at a time. The Holy Spirit is without measure (John 14:17).

The Holy Spirit Is *in* Us

He is in us for a new birth. We can accomplish the will of God because the power to perform His will is within us, the Holy Spirit (Ezekiel 36:25–28 NKJV).

The Holy Spirit Is *Upon* Us

The Holy Spirit is upon us for power (Acts 1:8 NKJV). This promise of divine power (dunamis) is called experiencing the fullness of the Holy Spirit for ministry. This uplifts after ministration. Whenever you are in the position of ministering, He comes upon you for the raw manifestation of His power (Acts 10:38 NKJV).

When we are in a deep relationship with the Holy Spirit, the glory of God is mightily manifested when we speak to people. We are speaking from the position where Christ has seated us—in heavenly places. The glory represents the weight of God's authority. Jesus taught us to pray in Matthew 6:10 (NKJV), "Your kingdom come. Your will be done on earth as it is in heaven."

When heaven's glory comes to earth, you can declare the kingdom of heaven is at hand. And when you do, even the forces of nature must bow.

I came across a story about a great man of God named John G. Lake, a missionary to South Africa in the early 1900s. It was said that many people in South Africa were dying of the bubonic plague, a dangerous and deadly virus. While assisting doctors during the plague, John G. Lake was asked why he had not contracted the disease since he used no protection. He said the spirit of life in Christ Jesus lives in him. John G. Lake demonstrated this when he had them take live bubonic-plague germs still foaming from the lungs of a newly dead person, put them in his hands, and then examine the germs under a microscope. The germs were dead!

The energy and presence of God were invisible to the naked eye but magnified under the microscope's lens. They proved to be a real, formidable, existing power that killed the virus. Here is how John G. Lake explained why he did not get sick:

he carried the cure in his body and spirit through the power of the Spirit through Jesus.

I heard David Herzog in a meeting giving this amazing testimony of John G. Lake. John G. Lake asked doctors to bring him a man with inflammation in the bone. He asked them to take their instruments and attach them to his leg while he prayed for healing. Then, he asked them what they saw taking place on their instruments. They replied that every cell was responding positively! John G. Lake replied, "That is God's divine science!"

All creation can hear, listen, obey, respond, and worship its Creator. Jesus commanded the fig tree to die, and the tree obeyed Him. Every living thing can and does respond because it was created with the capacity to hear and obey. Everything created can hear and respond, but the difference between the rest of creation and man is that the Holy Spirit is with us, the indwelling of the Holy Spirit in us and upon us. The walls of Jericho crumbled because the children of Israel shouted with praise. The power of the sound in their voices on that day carried greater power. There is a sound of God's glory that is released when we shout to the Lord corporately. True worship leads to the glory and presence of God appearing in response to worship. When the Lord in His glory shows up, every sickness and every demon flees. Words are spirit. You can speak life, or you can speak death.

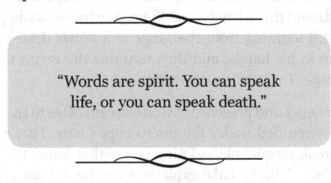

"Words are spirit. You can speak life, or you can speak death."

Psalm 141:3 (KJV) says, "Set a watch, O Lord, before my mouth. Keep the door of my lips."

Wow, he called your lips a door. This is an Old Testament request. God is not going to keep your lips. What God is going to do is He's going to show you how to keep your lips. The enemy would try to give you a situation where you would speak the wrong thing to paint a picture of doom. Their job is to get you to loosen your tongue and believe or say something that God didn't say. Paul teaches in Ephesians 4, "Let no corrupt communication come out of your mouth, but that which is good to the edifying that it may give grace to the hearers."

God wants you to speak words that will build up things, not tear them down. Let's go back to Job 3:35. Job had a battle with Satan himself. The devil inflicted Job with so much pain. I have heard people say, "Well, the Lord was testing Job." However, the testing accompanied what Job had set in motion. Job said in 3:25 (NKJV), "For the thing I greatly feared has come upon me." I believe fear was something that came into Job's life that started a sequence of activities. The fear of us thinking of what happens if we lose what we have at the present. And this is where we come up with backup plans.

Job's mouth got him in trouble. The Bible says that "for as he thinks in his heart, so is he" (Proverbs 23:7 NKJV). But I want to emphasize here that positive thinking alone is not going to deliver you. Why? Because your *words*, not your thoughts, have authority. Thank god for the positive thinking, for it's the first step to resisting and overcoming the spirit of worry. Positive thinking alone will not change your circumstances. Combining positive thinking and your oral declarations brings about change.

Jesus Heals a Centurion's Servant

Now, when Jesus had entered Capernaum, a centurion came to Him, pleading with Him, saying, "Lord, my servant is lying at home paralyzed, dreadfully tormented." And Jesus said to him, "I will come and heal him. The centurion answered and said, "Lord, I am not worthy that You should come under my roof. But only speak a word, and my servant will be healed. For I also am a man under authority, having soldiers under me. And I say to this one, 'Go,' and he goes; and to another, 'Come,' and he comes; and to my servant, 'Do this,' and he does it. When Jesus heard it, He marveled, and said to those who followed, "Assuredly, I say to you, I have not found such great faith, not even in Israel. Then Jesus said to the centurion, "Go your way; and as you have believed, so let it be done for you." And his servant was healed that same hour. (Matthew 8:5–10, 13 NKJV)

Positive thinking combined with word declaration under the leadership of the Holy Spirit produces power. Speak to that sickness in your body, speak to your lack, and declare what the Word says about your situation in Jesus's name. Believe and see it work. Your words have value. Every word that you speak, you must measure against the Word of God. In this world, the devil will try hard to put some pressure on you. You should be able and willing to see yourself in the future. Your future is now, and it's inside you. Tap the wells from within you and experience the manifest glory of God upon you.

"I will worship toward thy holy temple and praise thy name for thy loving-kindness and for thy truth: for thou has magnified Thy word above all thy name" (Psalm 138:2 KJV).

This scripture is talking about Jesus. Do you know what he did? He magnified His Word above His name. Let me tell you what that means. That means that if He ever speaks something, He surrenders to it.

He is under the authority of whatever He spoke to you, and we won't ever get Him to change. If He promised you something, He completely gives Himself to it. Don't worry, for God has your back. Worry opens demonic doors to attack your body and soul, giving demons the legal right to touch every area in your life. That's why Jesus admonished us not to worry or be afraid. Jesus Christ knew these demonic spirits would come after us; but we should not give them a chance by thinking, acting, or speaking contrary to the Word. The spirit of worry can saturate your mind so you don't experience your miracle. I encourage you to put on your dancing shoes and celebrate God regardless of the attacks in the mind and see Him assist you supernaturally.

Healing Miracles in My Life

Growing up, I never loved injections or syringes. My mom was a nurse back in Africa. She would carry us, lay us on her lap, and then inject a syringe in our buttocks whenever we were sick. That increased my hatred for needles even more as it was so painful. Thus, while I was growing up, the fear never left me.

I had to go to preach one evening. Unfortunately, I felt sick because of stress and work without rest. I prayed and asked God to forgive and heal me. I was suffering from an intense fever. I turned on the TV, soaking worship. This helped my mind to stay focused on God's healing over me. I believed and spoke healing over my body.

After praying, I fell sound asleep. As I slept, I had a dream where I saw a nurse walking through the door of the room.

The nurse was dressed in a style of clothing that was from the past, with their traditional cap. She held a syringe with a very long needle in her hands. The huge syringe petrified me, yet I could not move a limb out of fear. I was in a dream, but I still felt fragile in my body. As the nurse walked toward me with the large syringe, she smiled at me, and I smiled back. It only took a matter of seconds for her to inject the syringe into my side and pull out a nasty thing from my body. Then, she said to me, "You are well."

Immediately, I woke up from that dream, and I could feel that I was completely healed. It was only four in the afternoon when I opened my eyes, and I had to start the service at seven. That day, I was able to walk into that service and preach the gospel with so much energy and passion. That night, we saw multiple miracles of people being healed and turning to Christ. While I could have continued to worry, I chose to pray to Him instead, and God intervened. Not one ounce of worry could redeem me, but the blood of Jesus Christ did. I was optimistic in mind and declared with my mouth, believing in the Word of God, and it came through.

On another occasion, my wife and I lay down, preparing to sleep. I was lying there quietly when I began to feel the fire of God in my palms and under my feet. It was so intense that I had to take off the blanket and allow the air to cool me down, but the intense heat did not cool down. I did not know that my wife was sick. While I went to sleep, she stayed awake beside me. It was between 12:00 a.m. and 3:00 a.m. that she took my hands and placed them on her stomach. As she did, she felt fire moving from my hands into her stomach. In an instant, she was healed of her pain. My wife's mind was focused on receiving a miracle.

These healings took place not just in our lives but also in the lives of the people who attended our meetings. In all services, we have witnessed the strong presence of God touching the lives of the people who came with an expectation to receive. As the Holy Spirit permits, we have seen many miracles happen in worldwide services.

Creative Miracle

While I was ministering in Argentina, a woman who was to have surgery, potentially losing a leg, was wheeled into the service. She came, believing that God would heal her. After the message, we began to worship the Lord Jesus; and immediately, she was wheeled to me. I began to feel that intense fire that accompanied the anointing to heal. By the direction of the Holy Spirit, I placed my hands on her head, and she began to shake. The Lord stretched His hand to heal her, and she got up from her wheelchair. Thus, God performs mighty wonders on a wide scale. She came believing in God for her healing with a focused mind on Jesus Christ.

Tracheostomy Healed

There was another woman in Argentina who had a tracheostomy and lost her voice completely. She couldn't speak and was in pain. When she saw how the Holy Spirit healed a lady who was in a wheelchair, she ran to the front with her husband.

The husband was speaking, and my interpreter was translating for me. With the direction of the Holy Spirit, I placed my hands on her throat, and the power of God came over her. She went down to the floor supported by ushers. While praying for others, I heard my wife and others calling me. I turned and beheld this lady was up with her voice restored, and the pain was gone. She spoke with clarity. God created a new trachea!

While I was preaching in Pakistan for a great man of God, Pastor Anwar Fazal, we saw God open blind eyes and many other tangible miracles in the crowd of about six thousand. I was also scheduled to preach at his friend's church, which was located on the roof of a building. This church had about three hundred people who had gathered to worship the Lord.

As we entered, I was advised not to walk into the crowd while preaching because of security concerns. But at this moment, the Holy Spirit came upon me, and I began to walk through the crowd of three hundred people trying to stay in the aisles.

In the midst of the crowd, a lady who was suffering from continuous bleeding and could hardly walk sat. I walked among the people while preaching. On my way back to the front, we heard a shout from the back. A lady and those who assisted this lady into the service were jubilating and screaming. It drew my attention, and immediately, I asked what happened.

She told us that before the preacher had entered, she said to God she wanted the preacher to walk by her so she could touch his garment," and that was exactly what happened. She touched my clothes, and the power of God flowed through into her; she was instantly healed. She rejected being worried, frustrated, or depressed. She spoke to her family to carry her to church. She was carried up the roof, and Jesus Christ met her just at the point of her need. The bleeding completely ceased and was restored.

Quit worrying about your health. Focus entirely on Jesus Christ and see what He can do for you. I'll say this again: don't pray from a place of worry but a place of trust. God brought supernatural healing to her because of her faith. It was not the size of her sickness but the size of her faith in God that delivered her.

Encountering Jesus

Lastly, I had a dream while lying with my wife in the praying room. In my dream, I saw that I was in the living room. As I turned my view to the door leading into the garage. I saw a bright light, and from it came a set of feet with scars where the nails had pierced. Next, I saw that the living room around me

138

transformed into a field where little children played. I saw the Lord walk toward me, and I was overwhelmed with emotions. He held me around my neck and uttered three simple words, "I love you."

I cannot explain the joy I felt at that moment. However, I asked Him, "What about my wife? What do you have for my wife?"

He said, "I've done something great for her, and I'm going to visit her too." He walked through the guestroom where I was lying.

I could see myself and my wife lying down. As I opened my eyes, I saw my wife next to me, trying to wake me up. She said, "Honey, did you just see the light that went through the window?"

I said, "Yes, that was Jesus," and I told her everything that the Lord had revealed.

After that, I went back to sleep and had another dream where I saw another light coming toward me. Through this light came a person in all their beauty. However, I quickly discerned that it was the devil because the Bible states how He adorns himself in an attempt to imitate the glory of Christ. The devil came toward me, and I said, "In the name of Jesus, I rebuke you, whoever you are."

Immediately, this person changed, and it was the devil himself. He looked at me and said, "I am going to kill your mother-in-law."

I said, "No way! That is not going to happen!" And he disappeared. I spoke to my wife about it, and we prayed.

A week later, we got a call that my mother-in-law was extremely sick and was taken to the hospital. After a few minutes, the nurse made an error and almost gave her the wrong blood, but God intervened. She would have died if the wrong blood had been put into her. We witnessed the suffering of my mother-in-law when God intervened and healed her.

His supernatural healing is still at work, even at this age. All we need to do is to look to Him for help. Acts 3 (NKJV) includes a story where Peter heals a lame man who sits at the city gate, begging for money. Peter told him, "Silver and gold I do not have, but what I do have I give you: In the name of Jesus Christ of Nazareth, rise up and walk."

Peter told the beggar to look straight into his eyes and then commanded Him to walk. He was instantly cured. Peter directed the man to look at him because he wanted him to forget about his condition for a while and have faith.

Similarly, Jesus wants us to be focused on Him instead of our sickness when we pray. As we do this in faith, He heals us from our diseases. These miracles are still alive today. God is ready to liberate you from whatever you are suffering. Perhaps you are in the hospital reading this book or are suffering from some severe condition; just know that the healing angels of God are available right where you are. Call out to Him in faith, and He will set you free.

Thus, the Bible shows us three things we need to do to position ourselves for supernatural healing and creative miracles. Healing has to do with the process of time, while creative miracles are growing or replacing body parts instantly.

Repentance and Personal Acceptance of Jesus's Sacrifice

Acts 3:19 (NKJV) states, "Repent therefore and be converted, that your sins may be blotted out, so that times of refreshing may come from the presence of the Lord."

The first step into entering the realm of spirituality and activating the blessings of Jesus Christ for oneself is by accepting the fact that Jesus died for our sins. We must repent and be honest about our sinfulness so we can embrace the life of fulfillment Jesus offers through Himself.

Read the Word of God

"My son, give attention to my words; Incline your ear to my sayings. Do not let them depart from your eyes; Keep them in the midst of your heart; for they are life to those who find them and health to all their flesh" (Proverbs 4:20–22 NKJV).

The Bible tells us that humanity's survival is not dependent on food but on the Word of God. While earthly food feeds our bodies, the Word of God does so much more than that. It nourishes our soul and feeds our spirit; it heals us inside out. While medication and food help us in our natural bodies, the Word of God goes deeper to cure and restore us in every way. Therefore, we need to make God's Word our medicine that can cure every problem. Whether we are in emotional, mental, or physical pain, the Word can invade all our lives and perform wonders that no earthly remedy can.

Prayer

James 5:16 (NKJV) states, "Confess your trespasses to one another, and pray for one another, that you may be healed. The effective, fervent prayer of a righteous man avails much."

Therefore, one weapon that we see is prayer. As we pray with unwavering faith, we can claim our blessings situated in the heavenly realms. We can argue that Jesus's suffering was on our behalf; and by His wounds, all sicknesses must loosen their grip. The greatest weapons we can use against the devil are the Word of God and prayer because He knows these things increase our faith and mitigate the strength of his demonic forces. That is why we need to position ourselves for a miracle and prepare to battle against the evil one.

We are constantly surrounded by evil forces that are always scheming to make us worry and doubt God's ability to provide, heal, and restore. Our only hope is to fight the good fight. Be faithful in prayer and eradicate all doubt from our minds.

The truth is that most of us have a mindset that doesn't align with the Word. The world teaches us to rely on earthly healing. It makes us dependent on our abilities and man-made medications. That is why, when we see all these earthly remedies failing, we lose all hope for our healing. Especially in the case of fatal diseases, we often surrender to their consequences, thinking that we will never be able to witness healing again. Supernatural healing restores our hope. It shows us that when earthly means fail, we can access our blessings through the spiritual realm by the Spirit of God.

The Bible teaches us numerous examples of these supernatural healings where God healed the people who had no hope of being cured. Matthew 9:20–22 (NKJV) narrates an incident where a woman who has been bleeding for twelve years finally receives her healing. It is written:

> And suddenly, a woman who had a flow of blood for twelve years came from behind and touched the hem of His garment. For she said to herself, "If only I may touch His garment, I shall be made well." But Jesus turned around, and when He saw her, He said, "Be of good cheer, daughter; your faith has made you well." And the woman was made well from that hour.

Similarly, Luke 13:11–13 (NKJV) recounts an incident of a woman who was crippled for eighteen years, and Jesus healed her: "And behold, there was a woman who had a spirit of infirmity eighteen years, and was bent over and could in no way raise herself up. But when Jesus saw her, He called her to Him and said to her, 'Woman, you are loosed from your infirmity.' And He laid His hands on her, and immediately she was made straight, and glorified God."

The Bible describes many other incidents where people were healed supernaturally and even brought back to life from the dead. These events show God's divine power to heal people. As Jesus healed them or used His disciples to display His authority and power, He showed us that there was nothing He could not do with the anointing of the Holy Spirit through prayer and fasting. These miracles might have happened two thousand years ago, but the blood of Jesus is still available for our healing. We can pray and claim health for ourselves. However, the problem is that humans do not recognize their power and authority. Instead, they allow the devil to drown them in doubt and fear. We embrace negativity instead of creativity and a positive mindset. That is what keeps us from receiving God's blessings already sealed for us in the heavenly realms.

Therefore, we need to change our perception and instead focus on being steadfast and positive about our health. We need to recognize that God is our Father, and He is interested in healing His people. He had never intended to leave us on our own. He created us to live lives of fulfillment and blessings. That is why we need to step outside the earthly perspective and instead reflect on the promises of God. That is how we can access His favor, mercy, and grace.

For many, ill health has become an undefeatable monster, a Goliath that can't be knocked down. We look at the size of our sickness and not at how great our God is. We must remind ourselves that God can do exceedingly great things in our lives. We know that with our God, nothing is impossible. Therefore, once we give Him the glory in every circumstance, He will take control, bringing glory to His name through our lives.

Today, this power is available to us because the Spirit of God still works in us. I believe that this is the hour and time when the world needs to see the great manifestation of the power of God in our lives. As sons and daughters of God, anointed by His Spirit, we can be the source through which they may see the power of God—the supernatural healing God provided in your life. Have the right mindset. Speak positively, think positively, and act positively.

9

❖

Experiencing God's Glory

History is filled with accounts of many revolutionaries who brought about a change with just one thing: passion. When everything else failed, their unmatched determination and perseverance to accomplish their goals led them to their ultimate destination through the darkest of times. As a result of their contributions, these personalities have become sources of motivation for people worldwide.

However, while these people continue to lionize them, very few want to have the same passion and determination. Complacency and passivity have been embedded in our society, hindering us from accomplishing so much more than we have.

One of the main keys to experiencing the glory of God is passion. Passion for His glory eliminates worry and builds faith. "You will seek me and find me, when you seek me with all your heart" (Jeremiah 29:13 NKJV).

According to many successful people, passion has been one powerful trait that has helped them achieve great heights.

Successful scientists, CEOs, athletes, and film directors testify that their deep motivation drove them to work hard. That hard work eventually helped them succeed. Therefore, we know that passion is the secret ingredient to success in any area of life, and walking with the Holy Spirit is passion. However, passion is not only limited to worldly aspects but also to our relationship with God. It all depends on what choice we make for ourselves.

Therefore, in this chapter, we will study passion and its advantages and disadvantages. We will learn from examples of biblical characters that show us how the passion for God's glory is pivotal for our spiritual growth and how we must come out of the lukewarm mindset by becoming passionate followers of Jesus Christ. The enemy wants to cripple us with worry, but God has created us to live our lives to the fullest. We must not just be passersby in this journey of life but active participants in the grand project of spreading His image worldwide.

The word *passion* comes from the Latin word *passio*, which has the Greek root *path*, which means "to suffer." It is a powerful emotion that can control the mind and, thereby, our actions. Paul uses this word in Romans 1:26 (NKJV) when he says, "For this reason, God gave them up to vile passions." Here, the word *passion* comes from the Greek word *pathos*, which means "an affliction of the mind or emotions" or, in other words, "a feeling that the mind suffers from." It implies that it is always intense regardless of whether the passion is good or evil.

Passion is a strong and barely controllable emotion. The suffering and death of Jesus Christ is the best example of it. He was passionate about His goal to come on earth to die for our sins. Despite leaving heaven and receiving humiliation in man's hands, Jesus never lost His passion. He wanted to accomplish His purpose.

The Bible primarily uses the word *passion* to describe sinful desires. For instance, Paul states in 1 Corinthians 7:9 (NKJV), "But if they cannot exercise self-control, let them marry. For it is better to marry than to burn with passion."

He uses the word to describe the uncontrollable sexual urge that humans have as a part of their carnal nature. Once again, he uses it to refer to an uncontrollable emotion. But in Galatians 5:24 (NKJV), he tells us how these emotions are put to death when we accept Christ and begin a new life in Him. He says, "Those who are Christ's have crucified the flesh with its passions and desires."

That means evil passions no longer dominate our hearts and minds when we surrender to Christ. Instead, the former passions are replaced by a new passion: a burning zeal to love and obey God and save the lost. This passion stems from the Holy Spirit in us, who always encourages and motivates us. David talks about this heavenly passion or zeal in Psalm 69:9 (NKJV), "Because zeal for Your house has eaten me up, and the reproaches of those who reproach You have fallen on me."

He expresses how the desire for the house of God is so strong that it has overtaken him.

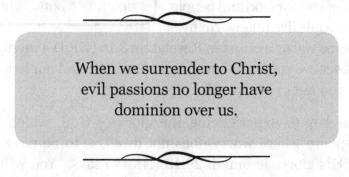

When we surrender to Christ, evil passions no longer have dominion over us.

While the devil entices us to pursue evil passions, the Holy Spirit instills a burning passion for God. There is a major emotional shift as we accept Jesus in our lives. Our goals and objectives change when we pursue God's will instead of our own without any fear of evil. As I mentioned, worry opens up fear, leading to discouragement. We all want to develop passion inside us, but the things around us restrict it and make us give in to fear. Starting a ministry or a new career will make you go around in circles because you

> There are two kinds of passions: godly passion and demonic passion.

don't know how to go about it. When we begin to overthink, we put ourselves in a place of fear or worry.

Unfortunately, as the devil struggles to stop us from following God, he strategizes to water down our passion for Him, if not completely end it. The devil knows that if we go after what God has planned for us, he will not be allowed to access our lives. Fear can rob us of God's promises of life and His goodness. Instead, we must get up and move forward in faith. Fear blocks out all of God's blessings and miracles and causes us to have confidence in the devil's ways. The church is a living example of passivity and a lack of zeal. The people are increasing in number with every passing day, but their personal lives are devoid of love for God and people. These people live lukewarm lives

> Passion is not simply an emotion but a force that compels you to get up and do something.

that Jesus warns against in Revelation 3:16 (NKJV) saying, "So then, because you are lukewarm, and neither cold nor hot, I will vomit you out of My mouth."

The key to experiencing the glory of God, which is an atmosphere where worry does not dwell, is to be passionate about His glory. Jeremiah 29:13 (NKJV) says, "You will seek me and find me when you seek me with all your heart."

We must seek God for help. He is our Protector and Sustainer, the only one we can trust and give all our worries.

This is made clear in Matthew 6:33 (NKJV), which says, "But seek ye first the kingdom of God and his righteousness, and all these things shall be added unto you."

Every man and woman needs to possess a great deal of passion for seeing heaven manifest in their lives and ministry.

We can't be passionate and still be seated, doing nothing at all. When you are passionate about something, you will run after it. For example, when I met my wife, I didn't just say "Hey, I love you" and stayed where I was. I had to do something like go after her to talk to her or draw her attention. It happens in every relationship; you pursue that which you want. A man will show that he is passionate about her by taking her out on dates, buying flowers and chocolates, and doing everything to draw her attention to him.

> Thus, intimacy is essential since it is considered a fruit of passion.

However, a couple of years later, the passion slowly disappears in married life, and routine and familiarity set in. They don't do what they once did before getting engaged, let alone getting married. In the same way, this relates to our relationship with Jesus Christ. At first, we will spend time praying and studying the Word, understanding God's works and ways, but we lose the passion over time.

We cannot confess our faith verbally and not manifest it in our actions. And this is what the Lord desires to see in His followers. He does not want people who merely talk but those who are passionate about following His Word and making Him known to others. One of the proofs of passion is that we need to go after what we want, even if it is to inspire someone. If we want to experience the glory of God, we need to go after it for His glory to manifest in our lives or family. This is how people become successful in life; they are passionate about what they intend to do.

The Bible gives us several examples of passionate people whom God chose for His glory. The Old Testament includes stories of people like Moses, David, and Elijah, who deeply loved God and His Word. Their love was not just a simple human emotion, but it was so strong that it set them apart from the people in their generation.

In the ancient scriptures of 1 Samuel 13:14 (NKJV), "The LORD has sought for Himself a man after His own heart." God bestowed upon David a special recognition, referring to him as a man whose heart resonates with the very essence of the divine. The words of the Lord echoed "Behold, I have discovered a man whose spirit aligns harmoniously with My own" because of his faith and passion for Him.

Similarly, in the New Testament, we see the disciples of Jesus who were so passionate about Him that they left everything they had and followed Him. Even after Jesus's ascension, they continued preaching the Word of God despite the persecutions and sufferings. That is the kind of passion that God searches for—the passion for knowing Him and seeking after Jesus and, most importantly, taking time to spend with Him daily.

When it comes to giving time, we become very selfish and forgetful. God has given us twenty-four hours in a day; the least we can do is give Him a tenth of it. Just imagine a world where every child of God gives just a tenth of their day to the one who gave them life. It will have a positive and fruitful impact on our lives, ministries, and families. The more we worry about worldly things, the more we will be prone to lose our passion. Just as a man and a woman give time to be intimate in marriage, we must also give time to God. Intimacy creates closeness. You get to know your partner more. Communication, intimacy, and understanding between partners are essential. He wants to bless us so we can experience a supernatural power like never before as we get to know Him intimately. Through intimacy with the Holy Spirit, He turns to reveal Jesus Christ and His mysteries to us.

In the Old Testament, the story of Obed-Edom gives us insight into what this passion looks like. As David and his thirty thousand men arrived, they placed the Ark of the Covenant on the carton. A man named Uzzah, who had the ark in his possession for many years, attempted to catch it when it began to fall off the cart. That enraged the Lord, and Uzzah died that very moment beside the ark of God.

One main way to experience God's glory is to study our manual. When we do not study our manual properly, we will mess up. The manual I am talking about here is the Bible, the ultimate manual to keep our lives on track to witness the glory of our Father. We are always ready to take shortcuts to get away with things. We fail to understand that shortcuts lead to problems, disasters, and troubles.

All this needs investment in the form of time. When we give time to our studies, we understand what we are reading. The same thing applies to understanding the Word. To understand God and His instructions, we must invest our time in the Holy Spirit.

As God's followers, we must always believe and follow our manual. When David neglected the manual in 1 Chronicle 13:7, he saw what happened. The ark was not meant to be carried on a new cart but on the priest's shoulders. The Philistines transported the ark on a cart in 1 Samuel 6:10–11. They got away with it because they were Philistines, but God expected more from His people. Because God's cause must proceed through the world through consecrated men rather than mechanical means, it was ordained that the ark be carried on the shoulders of the priests. We can imagine what these men thought. "Look, we have a new cart for the ark of God. God will be very pleased with our fancy new cart!" God has set a standard, and we must abide by those biblical standards to become carriers of His glory.

At first, David's dance meant nothing to God because he did not study and follow the right manual on bringing the ark of God into Jerusalem. We can dance, pray in tongues, and shout; but when we are not in the right standing with God or in the place of obedience, it's a waste of time. Such does not attract the manifestation of God's glory.

Petrified by this, David decided to keep the ark at the home of Obed-Edom, a Gittite. He must have been a man of faith to allow the ark in his home after God had killed someone for touching it. Obed means "enslaved person" or "outcast." He came from a city called Gath, which produced Goliath. He was a man who was never considered to come close and not talk of hosting the ark of God!

There will come a phase where we will feel rejected, disrespected, and unimportant in life for whatever reason. Despite all that, we should not lose hope as we are candidates to be blessed by an extraordinary being: our Father. Using our circumstances as an excuse for losing hope is not right. When the Lord looks over us, we should be passionate about facing difficulties and achieving what God has called us to do. Something good is bound to happen when we strive for His manifested glory.

Moreover, when we feel we are not qualified, we become the best candidates for Him. Our God will bless us when we least expect it. First Chronicles 13:14 (NKJV) says, "And the ark of God remained with the household of Obed-edom in his house

152

three months. And the LORD blessed the household of Obed-edom and all that he had."

The ark remained at Obed-Edom's for three months, during which the Lord blessed his entire household. In the glory, there's acceleration.

> ### Prayer Declaration
>
> In the glory of God, I prophesy to you that what will take you one year will take you one month. What will take you one month will take you one day, what will take you one day will take you one hour, and what will take you one hour will take you one minute. What will take you one minute will turn into seconds. In the glory, there's no time.

Because the ark of God was in Obed's home, everything multiplied. I came across an article known as the rabbinic literature, which states that Obed-Edom's wives and eight daughters-in-law had sixteen children during those three months. It's amazing what can happen in the glory. When the glory of God or His presence manifests unusually, it breaks worldly protocols. When the glory of God enters our lives, we will achieve things faster through His blessings.

The people told David, "The Lord has blessed the family of Obed-Edom so great. Everything in his house has experienced supernatural blessings. This is because the Ark of the Covenant of God was there." Obed-Edom honoring God's presence in his house provoked David back into action. This time, David read his manual correctly on how to bring the ark of God into Jerusalem. Psalm 24 is based on the ark as it ascended into

Jerusalem. David was thinking of the blessings that came upon Obed-Edom.

Obed became addicted to the presence of God; and when it came time to move the ark to Jerusalem—this time, correctly—Obed-Edom had a choice. He could have stayed where he was and lived off his past relationship with God and the blessings or moved with the ark of God, staying in God's presence and a relationship with God. Obed-Edom had a desire for the Lord and chose to move with God. Keeping in mind that Obed-Edom was an outcast, David was shocked to see the blessings and change in the house where the ark was. Furthermore, Obed-Edom became addicted to God's blessings so much that he took his family to Jerusalem when David brought the priests to carry the ark from his house.

His desire for the Lord caused him to do whatever it took to be close to Him. He had tasted firsthand the power of God's presence. When you have a genuine encounter with the glory of God, there's no turning back. Obed was so faithful in his service to the Lord that it resulted in supernatural promotions.

> If you can guard God's presence in your house, then you can do it in His house.

Why supernatural? Because in man's eyes and based on his status, he was not supposed to have hosted the ark of God. He was an outsider. Because of Obed-Edom's desire and love for the Lord and his faithfulness, God began to bless and promote him again. He became a

- gatekeeper,
- worship leader and musician,
- doorkeeper of the ark, and
- in charge of the whole temple's treasures.

In 1 Chronicles 26:15, he got to the north gate, and his sons looked after the storehouse. If you honor God in your home with your children, God will put you in a position of influence in the whole nation.

It begins at home.

Today, many people come into the church and are looking for the pulpit only because they believe that's where the encounter is. No! You will encounter God's presence in the area you are assigned to serve in the body of Christ. Stay faithful, and God will promote you.

Obed's welcoming behavior showed that he was a God-fearing man. He revered the Lord and accepted the ark without any objections. God also blessed him with eight sons, whom Obed named in honor of God's blessing as a reward for his attitude. He also had sixty-two strong male heirs who were also faithful and obedient to God. Obed's devotion and faith showed what true passion for God looks like and how God delights in such passions and rewards with countless blessings.

God favored Obed-Edom, and his family's lives were changed forever. God's favor in our lives will take us from the back to the front. It will put us among great men and women in society, as well as it will bless our lives. Accepting Jesus in any situation and evoking His glory will lift us from the chaos in our lives. Moreover, it will change people's perceptions of you. You will be promoted and successful as you serve Him with all your heart. Obed-Edom created a legacy of faith and relationship with the Lord through his faith, attitude, and actions. The Lord was faithful to Obed-Edom, establishing a legacy of generational blessings through his family bloodline. Because of his hosting God's presence, his name now had a completely different meaning. He was mentioned together with the Levites. Obed now means "the servant who honors God in the right way," and Edom is "one who causes to blush." He made David blush in shame because he was at first afraid to receive the ark, whereas Obed Edom took it into his house without hesitation.

Success needs to satisfy you internally. Money should not be our only criterion for success. Hollywood celebrities have a lot of money and fame. Yet we frequently hear the news of attempted suicide by these same celebrities. Some of them are so famous and doing well in the business, even in their old age. Still, something stops them from being spiritually happy. That is why God's presence in our homes and where we work makes a huge difference. Only in His presence will we find peace in God.

A similar story of passion is found in Luke 9:1–10 about a man named Zacchaeus, who was also driven by the passion for Jesus and wanted to catch a glimpse of Him. He was tired of hearing other people's testimonies and miracles. Zacchaeus decided to be a testimony and encounter this Jesus. Zacchaeus had to overcome the spirit of worry, fear, intimidation, frustration, and depression:

> Then Jesus entered and passed through Jericho.
> Now behold, there was a man named Zacchaeus,
> who was a chief tax collector, and he was rich.
> And he sought to see who Jesus was, but could
> not because of the crowd, for he was of short
> stature. So he ran ahead and climbed up into
> a sycamore tree to see Him, for He was going
> to pass that way. And when Jesus came to the
> place, He looked up and saw him and said to
> him, "Zacchaeus, make haste and come down,
> for today I must stay at your house." So he made
> haste and came down, and received Him joyfully.
> But when they saw it, they all complained, saying,

"He has gone to be a guest with a man who is a sinner." Then Zacchaeus stood and said to the Lord, "Look, Lord, I give half of my goods to the poor; and if I have taken anything from anyone by false accusation, I restore fourfold." And Jesus said to him, "Today salvation has come to this house because he also is a son of Abraham; for the Son of Man has come to seek and to save that which was lost." (Luke 19:1–10 NKJV)

Zacchaeus was a short man and could not see over the people. Zacchaeus struggled to see the Messiah as the crowd huddled around Him. Although it was convenient for him to stay behind and let the people move forward, Zacchaeus did something extraordinary. He did not care about his position in life, his friends' feelings, etc. He made up his mind to hurry, break through the crowd, climb a sycamore tree, and sit there to see Jesus. As Jesus passed by, His gaze fell on this small man sitting up in the tree, and He told him that he would come to stay at his house for that night. Joyfully, Zacchaeus came down and received Him. Passion caused Zacchaeus to do something that was outside the realm of the norm or culture. The testimonies of others were not enough. He must see Jesus for himself.

The crowds who had been surrounding Jesus all this time became angry. Why? The crowd gets jealous when God takes note of somebody with passion. Persecution is a mainstay of people of passion. I can imagine the people and even Jesus's disciples angrily saying, "I have been walking with Him for days, weeks, and months, and He never asked me to stay at my house!"

Let me put it this way: Zacchaeus was not a church member; he was not among the prayer warriors' team and had no leadership position! During Zacchaeus's first time in church, he did something extraordinary that drew the pastor's attention and became highly favored by the pastor, while others might have been in there for years and did not or ever have the privilege. His passion and hunger for God separate a man from many. They questioned why Jesus chose to go to his house when he was sinful. However, Zacchaeus immediately told Jesus that he would give away half of his possessions to the poor and return fourfold to the people he had taken by false accusation. Zacchaeus's honesty and passion had drawn the attention of Jesus to him. Zacchaeus's passion set him apart for Christ.

The Lord is not attracted to how we look physically or religiously but by how zealous we are for Him. Can we forsake our convenience and come to Him no matter how difficult situations seem to be? Can we step out of our comfort zones and prioritize His will over our own? All these questions determine whether we truly qualify to become passionate followers of Him. How hungry are you for His glory over your life, family, or ministry? Our religious display of commitment and piety doesn't move the heart of God, but passion does.

The truth is, without passion, we can't experience the glory of God in this life. Jesus says in Matthew 22:37 (BSB), "Love the Lord, your God with all your heart and with all your soul and with all your mind."

He does not simply say to love the Lord but emphasizes dedicating every area of our lives to love Him. True passion is required to become disciples of Jesus Christ. We need to follow Him not only by faith but also through our actions.

Zacchaeus's passion made him stand out among those following Jesus. His passion caused him to do something nobody else was willing to do, and it gained the attention of heaven! Zacchaeus's passion opened the door for Jesus to come to reside at his home, and from that day on, tradition says Jesus used his home as His ministry headquarters each time He visited

Jericho. Would you like your home to be the headquarters for the next move of the Holy Spirit in your region? What are you passionate about even when you walk into the house of God? Your passion will draw the attention of heaven.

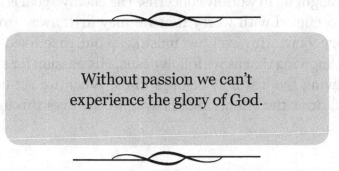

Without passion we can't experience the glory of God.

All those people who went on to follow Jesus did extraordinary things. Passion makes you go out of your way to do virtuous deeds in the name of God. As a result, you experience supernatural outcomes. Solomon is one of the best examples of doing something extraordinary. He gave thousands of gifts from his heart to God. The Lord came in his dream and asked what he wanted, to which he said he wanted wisdom. God's response was to make him wiser than any man alive. And God blessed him beyond his dreams because Solomon sought that which was spiritual, and every other thing was added to him (see 1 Kings 3:12).

As we take the first step toward living a passionate life for Jesus, our passion starts reflecting on how we spend every day of our lives. Our obedience, desire to worship God, and desire to preach His Word throughout the world demonstrate it. The Bible says that "for God so loved the world that He gave His only begotten Son, that whosoever believes in Him may not perish but have eternal life" (John 3:16 NKJV).

The Father's passion for a sinful world brought Christ to the earth, and Christ's passion for us led Him to the cross and death. But praise be unto Him that He also rose again and valiantly conquered sin and death on our behalf.

Our choice now is to live passionately for the Lord's gospel or be caught up in worldly concerns. The enemy's goal is to keep us so occupied with worry that we may drift away from our primary focus. However, we must keep our gaze fixed on the cross, knowing that as we follow Jesus, His passion for seeking and saving the lost now belongs to us. When we act upon it, we can draw the attention of heaven to our lives through this passion.

Angelic Encounter through Passion

I met an older woman in Indiana. After the service, she glowed. I told her that there was something different about her, and all she did was smile in return. However, I kept insisting that there was something different about her. She finally told me why she had that glow on her. She began by telling me that she worked as a church cleaner but was ninety years old at that time. Now, that caught me off guard as I could not believe it. You don't see many people in their nineties doing a job like that.

Nevertheless, she told me that she made sure that the church was kept clean before anyone entered the building. One day, as she was cleaning, she lifted her head and saw an angel, who spoke to her. Through that encounter, her household was saved. She had desired for all her children to be saved.

> Tears are a language that God understands.

It made me think that you can encounter God anywhere if you are passionate about Him. Your job descriptions in the church don't matter. You can do anything in His house, and just like the older woman, you can encounter Jesus. It was very similar to the story in 2 Kings 4:8–37, where the woman insisted Elisha eat food with her and her husband. This family prepared a room for Elisha each time he passed by. Eventually, Elisha went to rest in the house one day, sent for her, and asked what she wanted because of this great deed. Elisha's servant said she had no son, and her husband was old. So Elisha told her that next year, she would bear a son. Though she did not believe the word of Elisha, she conceived, and the power of God was revealed to her. This family's passion for serving brought about a tangible miracle in their family.

When it comes to our daily lives, you will see many people being blessed with great promotions. The only reason that they were granted such blessings was because of their passion for getting the task done. Whenever their boss gave them a project to do, they did it with great determination. Coming to work on time and doing their job passionately gave them a promotion. Pursuing a godly passion will unlock creative miracles in your life, family, and ministry. Trust God, no worries!

Passion unlocks revelation as it did in Mark 10:46–50 (NKJV), where Blind Bartimaeus encountered Jesus's blessing. It's said that he was the son of a rich man, but his condition made people reject him. In doing so, he will sit at the roadside to beg. I believe that Blind Bartimaeus had heard about Jesus and the great testimonies, and this time, he said he would be a testimony.

There was a large crowd and a lot of noise following Jesus. Instead of silently watching the Son of God pass by, Bartimaeus began screaming at the top of his voice, "Son of David, have pity on me!" The people sitting with him kept telling him to keep quiet, but his plea got louder until Jesus stopped and went to him. My beloved, your cry has been heard. Jesus is standing right where you are. You don't need to worry.

Jesus had heard it the first time, but He wanted to see how hungry and passionate Bartimaeus was to receive His miracle. When Jesus was pleased with his determination, He sent for him. Blind Bartimaeus immediately jumped up; left everything, including his garment; and ran toward Jesus. That garment identified his situation. He tossed it off, expecting to not need it anymore.

The time has come to throw away the bad garments that define us in society. The garment might have other meanings, such as us throwing away our old lives and anything that might keep us from serving Him wholeheartedly. In this sense, throwing the garment away was symbolic of Bartimaeus's desire to present himself to Jesus with an expectation of giving himself completely to the Lord Jesus. Throwing aside the garment was a literal decision to no longer rely on anything he might have relied on before as he came face-to-face with Jesus. Throwing aside the garment, he was choosing to trust Jesus to give him a better future, so much so that he was willing to let go of his most valuable asset: his only means of collecting alms to provide for his most basic needs. Beggars were defined as such by the cloak they wore. Usually, the cloak was the beggar's only possession and their only source of income. It was also the garment of shame.

Today, you see beautiful, godly ladies and handsome brothers, yet they are single and growing old! There's a garment covering them, not to be seen. When I was ministering, the Lord opened my eyes to see a woman with a dark garment covering her face. This lady had not been asked a hand in marriage. I called her to the front and rebuked that dark garment, and the power of God came over her, and she fell to the ground. The following day, a man out of the country was interested in her.

> ## Prayer
>
> In the name of Jesus Christ, every dark garment
> identifying you to the past or the current
> situation in your life, I rebuke, bind, and cast
> to hell now in Jesus's name. The garment of
> poverty, rejection, failures, and sickness, I bind
> you and cast you to hell in Jesus's name. The
> garment of shame and disgrace, I pull you off
> my head and cast you back to hell in Jesus's
> name! Jesus's blood has set me free. Amen.

The disciples brought Blind Bartimaeus to Jesus, and He asked him, "What do you want Me to do for you?" An open check! And he said, "I want to see," and Jesus touched him, and he was healed. His passion and determination produced a real miracle in his life. God has

> When Jesus is present,
> good things happen.
> He has your back.

released His angels to assist you without worrying about anything. Remember, each time you worry, you move backward from your breakthrough.

When we become the carriers of the presence of God, we will be able to do things that were first considered impossible. Being a Christian does not mean there will not be challenges. Problems will arise, and sometimes the situations can get so difficult to overcome that our faith may be shaken. Nevertheless, when we become glory carriers, every obstacle gives way to us. Whatever situations come before us, this honor of being carriers of God's presence will help us move forward. You might be down but not out. In an instant, Blind Bartimaeus goes from zero to hero. That will be your story, don't worry.

When we become the carriers of the presence of God, we will do things that were first considered impossible.

When you are passionate with your praise and dance before the Lord, it triggers His glory to be manifested in your life. Such actions produce supernatural results.

One of the best elders I ever had served the Lord, and they served us faithfully. Back in the day, he was hired as a janitor. He never went to school but studied independently and learned how to read. Striving to become educated, he continued to perform his janitorial duties while faithfully serving the Lord. He loved to dance and praise God even while working. Someone saw that he was faithful and passionate about his job. He was always on time and diligent. He was promoted to manager because of his hard work and dedication—by-products of passion. Today, he is retired, blessed, and highly respected in the community. He would have still been struggling if he hadn't been passionate about his janitorial job. His passion led him to be noticed and promoted in the same company as a general overseer without any school certificates. We must be faithful and committed to the assignment in our lives because it draws out favor from heaven. We can overcome and accomplish anything we want by leaving all our worries and following God.

10

---◆❖◆---

It's Not about
the Storm

The word *storm* points to our typical worldly problems. For example, not having a proper job, not completing graduation or achieving any goals, trying hard to maintain a relationship with a friend, and coping with pressure are all "storms." Troubles come at an unexpected time and rate. It depends on each individual how much they allow these problems to affect their lives. When our thinking needs to be reframed, our hearts are often confused about the future and whether we will come out of it or not. We will always go through tests and trials in our lives, marriage, home, and every area of life. We cannot escape it, yet we always try to run away from it. Problems, trials, and misjudgments were so common back in the early church's days. A thought process similar to this exists today, where we all face a problem that does not seem to be solved easily, quickly, and even end.

> On the same day, when evening had come, He
> said to them, "Let us cross over to the other side."
> Now, when they had left the multitude, they took
> Him along in the boat as He was. And other little

boats were also with Him. And a great windstorm arose, and the waves beat into the boat, so that it was already filling. But He was in the stern, asleep on a pillow. And they awoke Him and said to Him, "Teacher, do You not care that we are perishing?" Then He arose and rebuked the wind, and said to the sea, "Peace, be still!" And the wind ceased and there was a great calm. But He said to them, "Why are you so fearful? How is it that you have no faith?" And they feared exceedingly, and said to one another, "Who can this be, that even the wind and the sea obey Him!" (Mark 4: 35–39 NKJV)

"Be anxious for nothing, but in everything by prayer and supplication, with thanksgiving, let your requests be made known to God; and the peace of God, which surpasses all understanding, will guard your hearts and minds through Christ Jesus" (Philippians 4:6–7 NKJV).

Jesus is with you in the storm. Say, "Jesus is with me in this storm." Know that you are not alone. You are never alone. Your family is not alone. The eyes of God are open and watching. I want you to know it's not about the storm. Don't focus on the problems; focus on the promise. Hold on to the promise that God has spoken to you. Remember, He has said, "I am taking you to the other side. I will bless your family. I will prosper you. I will use you." He has said in His Word you shall be the head and not the tail. He has said in His Word that what your hands touch shall be blessed. He says you are blessed when you go out and come in. He says He will bless what you eat. He will bless what you drink. Hold on to His promise. He has said, "I am taking you to the other side. I am going to be with you." The Word of God has been spoken. He has said it, and will He not do it? Why worry?

It is left to you and me to decide what we do with or in the storm. Only you and I can cause a delay in the storm. For example, I was so excited when I got into high school. I'm a big guy. I'd be moving from one class to another, studying biology, geography, chemistry, physics, and advanced math. I was so excited but never knew that a time would come when I had to take an essay, not multiple choices. I've come to realize we are very excited during the first stage of any achievement. We put on our dancing shoes and dance until we get to the middle, and then we are, like, "Lord, is this what you intended for me? Is this what I signed up for?" Then, when they give back the exams, and you realize you passed, the excitement is even greater. When you overcome any situation in life, it's your happiest moment.

You enjoy the benefits when you stay put and cross to the other side. Listen, my dear friend, if you focus too much on the problems, you will lose sight of the promise. Don't focus on the problem. Don't focus on the situation. Don't focus on the storm or how big the storm is. How strong the winds are. The more you focus on the problem, the bigger the problem becomes, and the less you see the power of God. Let your focus be on Jesus Christ.

When I speak from a general point of view, being anxious about things is very common. Sometimes it can cause us to regret the actions we took in haste instead of having faith in God to do what he said in his Word! We already put so much on our plates that it becomes impossible for us to find a solution to everything. Our minds always think about ditching the idea when it is too late. The only solution that works all the time is prayer, which is what Mark 4:35–39 (NKJV) states. We must open our hearts and minds to God and request Him to give us the strength and understanding to deal with problems. We must show gratitude to Him through prayer. Prayer is the medium of establishing a connection with God. That is the straightforward explanation given to us more than a hundred times. Directing our attention to God when we struggle makes our anxiety drop so much that it provides us hope and peace. This peace comes from acknowledging that He is there for us every step of the way. In addition to gaining peace, we receive the support of a firm hand that can guide us through any storm.

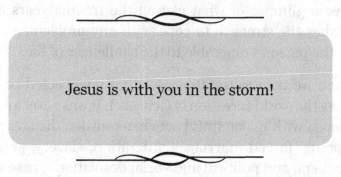

Jesus is with you in the storm!

Most people are going through or have experienced trauma. What may feel small or unimportant to us might be very traumatizing for the broken and suffering person. Some miseries affect an individual so deeply that they need help to come out of it. Unfortunately, they don't have many people around to understand that need. You may be distressed if you have experienced a stressful or disturbing event that has left you feeling emotionally abandoned and out of control. Emotional trauma can have you struggle with disturbing emotions, memories, and worries that will not go away. It can also leave you feeling emotionless, disconnected, and unable to trust others.

It can take a while to get over the agony when bad things happen. It is challenging to feel safe again. It's not the objective conditions that define whether an event is agonizing but your subjective emotional experience of the incident. The more frightened and deserted you feel, the more likely you will dive deep into the effect.

Worse is when trauma is left unhealed and stays with the affected person as they grow from childhood into adulthood. When children carry their suffering into their adulthood, it becomes hard to heal it. It affects their mental growth, and they quickly develop depression by facing a series of lingering problems that could have been handled on the spot. Some people find it hard to trust other people or themselves when they see a glimpse of what caused the trauma years ago. It diminishes the strength to cope with any problem, and that makes the person vulnerable to the challenges of life.

When we turn to the Bible, we find unexpected passages following the world's creation in Genesis 1. It was never a smooth experience with major sinful acts like murder, disintegration, kidnapping, forced marriages, migration, slavery, genocide, cannibalism, and political and social desolation. These events started in Genesis 4 and carried on up to the prophets. Moreover, the prophets that God chose to prepare the people for the arrival of His Son also had a tough time preaching the good news. Still, it did not stop anyone from fulfilling their objective.

> Nothing can stop you from getting to the other side except yourself. Stay faithful in the storm because it's not about the storm.

We live in a messed-up world where awful things can happen even to godly individuals. Anything from mishaps to misfortunes, disappointments, misuses, or even demise can be encountered. However, we can still trust Jesus Christ, realizing He has beaten our torment and injury. Only He can heal us of psychological and mental hurt.

"These things I have spoken to you, that in Me you may have peace. In the world you will have tribulation; but be of good cheer, I have overcome the world" (John 16:33 NKJV).

Jesus revealed to His disciples that we would confront endless trials because of what this world is. The wrongdoing and brokenness of this world create the catastrophes we encounter each day. Nevertheless, God guarantees freedom from the injury and hurt we may face in this present age. Even though there is distress and grieving today, God brings kindness in the morning. Thus, we wake up fresh and recharged. God brings healing to the physical body, mind, and spirit. He is, in fact, our Jehovah Rapha, which means "Jehovah who heals," who delivers us out of any pain and makes us one in Christ. What God has purposed and destined for you must come to pass. Are you with me? God's Word will not fail. It will never, never fail. God has a destiny for you.

Satan planned to destroy Moses just as he planned to destroy us. Luckily, God had planned the deliverance of the children of Israel. Satan, knowing God's plan, decided to kill the sons in the city. Listen, Moses being placed in a basket and left in the river was a setup for God's divine purpose. Whatever you might be going through at this moment, whereby you may feel like you have been placed in the basket and left in the dark waters of life, don't worry. It's a setup for your breakthrough.

Because she did not want her child to be killed, a mother's faith put the child in the basket and put it in the river. The Holy Spirit pushed the basket to the enemy's camp, and the enemy brought up Moses. Listen to me, people of God. Sometimes your enemy may try to hurt you, but God will use them to bring you up and bless you. It will work out to your advantage. Be patient and see what the Holy Spirit will do. It's not about the storm. Moses's mother didn't focus on the storm of babies being killed. It was difficult for her to place Moses in the basket. She looked beyond the storm and trusted God.

It's not about the storm—it's
about the plan of God!

Wow, glory to God! It's not about the storm. God will use your enemy to raise you well. For the people who don't like you, God will use them to feed you well. God will put you in their midst so that they will favor you. He did it for Moses. He did for the children of Israel, and the Word of God says, "He prepares a table before me in the presence of my enemies." As you are eating, your enemies will be watching in defeat. God will not put you where you enjoy the blessings in hiding. No no no! God will reward you openly, so many will come to believe in the Lord Jesus Christ through you. It's not about the storm. It's where God is taking you. Don't accept discouragement.

When Jesus is in the boat, you can tell the devil, "Bring it on. I know who I am. I know Christ will save me. I know the angels of God surround me. I know that Jesus is in my boat." At this moment, if you haven't, please invite Jesus into your boat because, with Jesus in your boat, your boat will not sink. The storm will come. As the Bible says, water came into the boat during the storm. Did you know Jesus would have walked or taken a different route and walked to the other side?

You see, whatever the Lord is doing, He has a plan. Look at the children of Israel. Here's the scene. When they left Egypt, Moses knew the route to the Promised Land. What happened on his way with Israel's children to the Promised Land? God met him and told him to make a U-turn; from there, God took them to a dead end. The U-turn took them to the Red Sea. I can imagine Moses arriving at the dead end and saying, "Whoa, God, I know the path to the Promised Land. I know the way. I had planned it out. I had worked it out."

Some of us plan and work things out instead of following God's plan. We used to sing a song, "Jack and Jill went up the hill to fetch a pail of water. Jack fell and broke his arm, and Jill came tumbling after." You can have a perfect plan. Then, God comes and reroutes you, and all of your plans are shattered. Moses was redirected. In front of them was the sea, and behind them was the enemy; they didn't know whether to go right or left. Sometimes God would allow the perfect storm to put you in a place where all you can do is rely on Him, and all you have is the last word He spoke to you.

The people were worried and afraid. They cried and shouted, "Moses, have you taken us out to destroy us? Look how the enemy is behind us, and in front of us is a sea."

The Bible says Moses cried to the Lord, "Oh, God!"

God responded, "Shut up. Be quiet. Why are you crying to me?"

God said you've got to know who you are in the storm. He wanted to show the people of Israel and their enemies that "I Am still the God in your storm." God asked Moses, "What is it that you hold in your hand?" God had the power to open the sea, but God always requires us to do something in the storm. He needs you; He needs me. "Moses, what are you holding in your hands?"

"Oh, I've got a rod."

"Remember, I gave you the rod. Take the rod and touch the waters."

Take that Word God has placed in you. You have a gift, a talent that God has given you. Take it. Use the Word of God and touch the waters in your storm. Use the Word of God to speak in your storm. Use what God has deposited in you in your storm.

The Bible says Jesus Christ was tired after ministering. Jesus and the disciples got into the boat, and Jesus said, "Let us go to the other side." They encountered a storm in the middle of the Sea of Galilee on their way. These were professional fishermen; they lived by the Sea of Galilee all their lives and made their living on the sea. They had gone through storms before, but this one was extraordinary. They had never seen this kind of storm before. Yes, during this tumultuous storm, Jesus was asleep! When He said, "Let's go to the other side," He looked for His pillow and slept comfortably in a corner. He was so deep in sleep while water kept coming into the boat, and the disciples were screaming; He continued to sleep.

Listen to me, friends of God. During the storm, God wants us to rest because resting produces strength. That's very important. When you are in a place of rest, you are being strengthened. You can think straight when you rest. You can do well when you rest. Statistics have shown that children who return from school and take a nap tend to do well in their education because their minds are in a state of rest; they can think and store information with clarity. The Bible says Jesus rested in a storm, and the Bible says the disciples cried out, "Teacher, you do not care that we are perishing?" And what did Jesus do?

The Bible says He arose, rebuked the wind, and said to the sea, "Peace. Be still." He was in a place of rest, and when He woke up from the place of rest, He woke up with strength and boldness.

When we are in the storm, and there is no rest, we tend to forget the power God has placed in us. We accept the spirit of worry, fear, frustration, depression, isolation, and even suicide. Here, we learn from Jesus that we have to rest amid the storm. He used what He had, which was the Word. God has given each one of us His Word. Speak the Word in the storm; hold on to the Word of God because it's not about the storm.

Did you know that God chose you? You didn't choose Him. You've heard people say, "You know what, I've found the Lord." He wasn't lost. We were lost; He found us. I don't need to know what you have been through. You might have had many things going on in your past. You might have been in jail or married five times, but you know what, that didn't change God's mind about you. He knows your potential. He put something in you. You couldn't have come into this world without the Holy Spirit giving you life, so He's got a plan for you. You are special. You have been chosen for such a time like this.

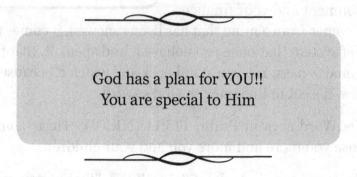

God has a plan for YOU!!
You are special to Him

When Satan came to Eve, he came after her thoughts. It's called the power of suggestion. You have to evaluate a thought once you think it because if it's not lining up with the Word, you do something with it. You cast it out. You can seal your mind. You can say, "In the name of Jesus, I take the blood, and I seal the door of my mind from that thought ever coming back again!" That thought cannot get back in. Use the Word of God, think positively, and declare the Word from a place of rest.

Matthew 12:34–35 says, "O Generation of vipers, how can you being evil, speak good things? For out of the abundance of the heart, the mouth speaketh." Watch this next one: "A good man out of the good treasure of the heart, brings forth good things" (KJV).

Here is that same verse in the Amplified translation, "You offspring of vipers. How can you speak good things when you are evil [wicked]? For out of the fullness, the overflow, the superabundance of the heart, your mouth is going to speak. A good man from his inner treasure brings forth good things." Everything comes from your inner man.

Jesus went around the world's system. He was producing everything from the kingdom. You too are in another system. You're in the kingdom's system. Don't worry; rest and declare the Word as Jesus did. You can speak the Word only and change your environment and your finances.

> It's not about the size of the storm; it's the size of your God.

But it comes from a mind that has been renewed. It comes from a belief system that once you believe it and speak it, that thing will come to pass. You can stand back and watch it because that is a law. It's got to line up with God's Word.

His Word says in Psalm 115:14 (NKJV), "He is going to increase you more and more you and your children."

His Word says in Isaiah 53:5 (NKJV), "By his stripes, you are healed." If Satan is coming to you with a thought apart from God's direction, cast that thing down!

The news is full of negativity, and if you stay tuned to it, you will find yourself in a state of worry. Worry can lead to health issues in your head, brain, nerves, and so forth. You need to tell Satan and yourself, "I've got the Word of God, and it is medicine to all my flesh" (Proverbs 4:20–22 NKJV). When you use the Word as medicine and take a dose every morning and evening,

> You didn't know how to dance, but you learned how to dance when the storm came.

the first thing that will change is your soul. Your soul will get right with God; when it does, that power will go from your spirit through your soul and hit your body.

I'm talking about people who don't have anything and have completely lost hope. You've been rejected because of the storm, and you don't think God can fix it. I've got news for you. God is still God. He can fix the worst situation. Whatever your problem is, God can fix it. Don't lose faith in your marriage, family, job, or school. You're going over, not under.

Jesus rebuked the storm, and it ceased. He turned and asked His disciples, "Don't you have faith?" In every situation you go through, God wants you to have faith. And in most situations, when a storm comes, it will build faith.

You didn't know how to pray, but when the storm came, you learned to pray. You didn't know how to read your Bible, but when the storm came, guess what, you're reading every chapter, every page. When the storm hits hard, you do the most extreme fasting of your life. You wake up at 3:00 a.m. and pray until 7:00 a.m. for a breakthrough.

The storm is a place to encounter God. The enemy might be laughing and saying, "Oh, I'm going to destroy you. I will destroy your family. I will destroy your marriage. I will destroy them all." Satan will work hard to see that you do not amount to anything in life.

The cross was the perfect storm for Jesus Christ. Men and others were delighted. They thought they had dealt with this man, Jesus. The devil was elated because he thought, *We've got him now! We have destroyed this Jesus Christ.* But Satan and his demonic agents didn't know that Jesus Christ would resurrect or come out of the perfect storm they had created.

Know who you are. Know that you are not alone in the boat. Jesus is with you in the boat, and when Jesus is with you in the boat, the boat will not sink. Water will come in; it might shake, but it will not sink—no need to worry.

You might be reading this book, and your boat is almost full of water to the extent that it's just your head that is above water. Maybe the water is just about to get up to your nose. But as long as you have Jesus and know who you are in Him, you will not sink. You're not going to die in the storm. You will come out powerful because it is not about the storm. You are with the powerful Man that even the sea and the winds obey Him when He speaks.

Satan brags by saying, "There is no way you will come out of this. I'm going to make sure you die in this storm." But he does not know that what he has orchestrated for you will result in a "God encounter," and His glory will manifest in your life.

Listen, friends of God, God wants to do something extraordinary on your behalf. Why is it not about the storm? Because Jesus was on assignment, and the storm was a distraction sent to get Him off course. But Jesus knew how to take His thoughts captive and put them to rest during the storm. Your mind plays a large part in the outcome of the storm.

Let's talk a little about the mind or mindset. What you accommodate in your mind during the storm will determine how long you will spend in the storm. What you are going through is based on the condition of the mind. Moreover, while we make a place for God in our hearts, He also wants to be present in our minds. Our mind is where we make decisions and develop our thought processes.

"Keep your heart with all diligence, For out of it spring the issues of life" (Proverbs 4:23 NKJV).

We are given a gift from God that we can't live without; our responsibility is to safeguard it with our lives. In Proverbs 4, the word *heart* represents our minds. It is critical to guard our minds in times of despair since it is a powerful weapon. For example, if someone is in poverty and becomes rich in the future, they will thank their positive minds for it, not education. While that may sound shocking, this is a revelation from the Holy Spirit. The Holy Spirit will reveal specific ways for you to overcome the problem you are in; it is up to you whether you avail yourself of that opportunity.

> Our minds are not created to store only information but to be creative. When you keep storing information, you lose creativity.

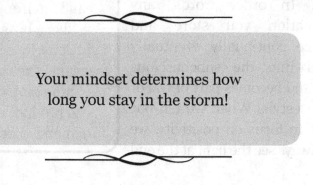

Your mindset determines how long you stay in the storm!

We make decisions daily, and our minds are always involved in that activity. We never know the time and place when we will encounter a test of our decision-making skills. I came across a study that indicated that 90 percent of what we do is done by the subconscious mind, whereas a conscious mind does 10 percent. When any information is given to you, it goes straight to the conscious mind. It will add to your subconscious mind if it stays in your conscious mind long.

For example, when anyone teaches you something, such as driving a car, the basic lessons and rules begin to develop in your conscious mind. As you learn more about it or talk about it, that lesson eventually becomes part of your subconscious mind. Therefore, the next time you drive anyone else's car or have to teach someone, you will know precisely what they need to know about the basics.

Whenever an idea or thought comes to your mind, it is best to write it down. The Bible says,

Let the weak say I am strong.

Let the poor say I am rich.

Let the blind say I can see.

If it stays long enough in your conscious mind, information will drop into your subconscious mind. In order words, any information you store and practice continually eventually moves into the subconscious mind and becomes part of you or your lifestyle. When we tell our minds to focus on positivity, we will always see the light at the end

Your conscious mind (your activity and environment) is like a boss. Your subconscious is like a servant. The conscious mind employs it to produce every demand or request.

of the tunnel. Those who are poor, blind, or weak or face problems that make them feel insignificant should believe in the Holy Spirit by acknowledging the power He has placed in them. Thinking positively is the first step toward progress out of misery.

We are the product of our subconscious mind, and this part of the mind makes us who we are today. If anyone tells us that we are sick or ill, and we agree with their words, then we will be sick. Furthermore, we live according to what we know and what we accept. If we accept that there is no other way out or that the outcome will always be wrong, we allow a negative mindset to run our lives.

Hence, the power of positive thinking is paramount, especially if we hope to see God's miracles in our lives.

Your subconscious will never forget, even if you forget. The information you receive growing up affects you positively or negatively. For example, in a family where everyone talks about poverty, drugs, abuse, etc., those negative concepts take residence in the subconscious. Some say we were born like this and will die like this. Where you were born and the people you surround yourself with matter. All these come into play when you are in the storm of life. The things you saw or heard when you were growing up form your outlook in life.

- What were your parents or guardians saying as you were growing up?
- What were they doing?
- How did they dress?
- What did they cook and how?
- What language was spoken at home?

Your environment influences your subconscious mind and helps create who you are today. The Bible says, "As a man thinketh in his heart so is he" (Proverbs 23:7 KJV).

You are the product of your subconscious mind. God spoke to Abraham to look as far as he could see, and it will be given to him. "As far as you can see, I will give it to you" (Genesis 13:14–15 NKJV). Can you conceive it? It is all about the mind, so what do you see?

> Doctors say if you can cheat your mind, you will be well.

What You Permit, You Become

I heard of a story concerning two individuals, Joseph and Jake. Both Joseph and Jake went to the hospital. Tests were done on both of them. Jake was told he had cancer and only had six months to live. Jake was given a clean bill of health. The twist here is this: the doctor mistakenly gave Jake's report to Joseph while Joseph's report was given to Jake. Jake, who had cancer but didn't know it, left joyful and excited. Joseph, who was in good health, became sad and discouraged because of the diagnosis of cancer that he was given. The report messed with his mind. Guess what? He eventually got cancer and died within those six months, while Jake was healed because of joy and peace of mind. So how you take information in your storm of life determines whether you will come out or stay there.

If poverty is in the subconscious mind, how can we treat it? Giving money to the poor never solves the issue. It's getting into their minds. It's a change of mindset. If you have not addressed the mind, you won't see success.

Your subconscious mind, the servant, is not as intelligent as your conscious mind, the boss. You can get sick simply by being told you are sick. The subconscious produces in the body the information it receives from the conscious mind. Jesus could control His mind in the storm. That is why He rested in the storm, woke up, and spoke to it. He was on an assignment. Jesus Christ was sleeping in the storm because a man was waiting to be set free on the other side. Mark 5 (NKJV) talks about this man who was possessed and filled with demons. The Bible says this man was so possessed that he would break every chain they would put on him. But Jesus was going to the other side because He was on a mission to set that man free. Remember, when Jesus met this demon-possessed man, he asked, "How many of you?"

The demonic spirit in the man said, "We are legion." A legion is a large number, between three thousand and six thousand. You can imagine three thousand to six thousand demons in one person. They wrapped themselves around that person's soul, causing chaos in his life and confusing his mind and thoughts.

Jesus was on a mission to set a man free. That is why it was not about the storm. It was about His purpose and assignment for that day. It was about destiny. It was about setting someone free. It was about Him doing what He had been called to do. The storm came. "Yeah, though I walk through the valley of the shadow of death." I will do what?

> A premature harvest means we don't realize the full potential or capacity of the fruit we desire.

I will fear no evil, for who is with me? For God is with me. Jesus went to the other side to set that man free.

God said He is taking you to the other side. Though you are going through a storm right now, it's not about the storm. It's about your assignment on the other side. Stay comfortable and rest in God's presence because you will fulfill what He has called you to do. Where? It is on the other side.

Look at the situation that took place. Jesus and His disciples were hungry, and Jesus told them to look for food. He said, "I need to go through Samaria." There was a storm known as hunger, but He was on assignment and needed to go through Samaria because He had to meet a lady to change her life. Jesus was so consumed with His assignment and goal that He did not focus on the storm, problem, or situation surrounding Him. He knew who He was. He knew the Holy Spirit was with Him. Sometimes, because of hunger, we lose track of everything. We may turn and curse everybody around us. We may turn and say, "Woman, I am not going to do this. I'm not going to go to church because I've not had my breakfast." Or you may say, "Since I don't have dinner, you know what, I need to go to the market and buy some stuff. Pastor, I'm not coming to church today because I'm going to get some food." You have to put aside distractions to accomplish your purpose. How many of us can put aside the distractions in the storm, knowing that it's not about the storm? It's where God is taking you. Focus on the goal, the prize.

Don't whine in your storm. Speak to it! Speak to the problem. Speak to the situation. Bask yourself in the presence of God. Build a strong intimacy with Jesus even in the storm because that is where the miracle occurs. The enemy's goal is to distract you using the storm and keep you there for as long as he can. But it's not God's will or purpose that we stay in the storm for a long time. Let's develop the right character. Let's develop the right attitude, which leads to the right behavior while in the storm because it's not about the storm; it's about the assignment God has given to you.

> Being spiritually blind is more unbearable than being physically blind. That is because the realm of the spirit is the actual reality.

Don't whine in your storm,
SPEAK TO IT!

Don't Give Up

"And let us not grow weary while doing good, for in due season, we shall reap if we do not lose heart" (Galatians 6:9 NKJV).

The reward that comes from God takes time. While we patiently wait for the reward, we should not allow discouragement or worry to affect us. In due time, the seed of our deeds that we sow with efforts will bear fruit. Regardless of the number of seeds we plant at one time, each will produce a harvest on its own time. That is one truth that we have to accept. If we get greedy or impatient and try to reap the harvest or reward earlier than its time, it will lead to great disappointment. When we disrupt a harvest, we destroy the gift that is being made ready for us. Nobody can ever be too prepared for anything, especially when it comes to dealing with tough times. We each experience hardships, regardless of how strong, confident, or powerful we are. Remember, the Word says, "Many are the afflictions of the righteous, but the Lord delivers him out of them all" (Psalm 34:19 NKJV).

The graph of our lives constantly fluctuates where we feel upbeat and jolly one day and then dazed and confused the next. While we think that finding a solution is the hardest thing about encountering tough times, we forget that not giving up is more critical and often more difficult. No greater and more powerful being exists than the one who created the world within six days. If He is the one who sustains and protects us from the works of the enemy, He will also be the one to reward us with things we could only dream of having in this life. When we put God first in our lives, we are rewarded ten times more, especially when our hearts and intentions are pure.

All of us are brought into this world for a reason. Christianity has always emphasized patience, unconditional love, and forgiveness whenever someone hurts us. As a matter of fact, that's how Jesus lived on earth. He was the ideal example of how God wants us to live. It may sound easy, but with constant disappointments and problems, we run away from the reward that awaits us.

We will find that we lack a clear picture of how to lead our lives in the right direction when we look deep within ourselves. However, this is not just typical blindness, like someone kicking dust in our eyes. This kind of blindness affects our lives as Christians. Hence, this is called spiritual blindness. People continue to turn away from God because they expect much from Him and seemingly get nothing in their requested time.

> Burnout is only permanent if you allow it to be. Do not listen to everything that you are tempted to believe when you are exhausted.

The opening of our eyes will be the silencing of our fears. In the dark, we are most likely to be frightened. The clearer the sight we have of the sovereignty and power of heaven, the less we shall fear the calamities of this earth.

When we have the Spirit of God in our lives, especially when it comes to good times, we are not prone to any fear. When we trust God, we can come out of any situation spiritually unharmed, and that helps us move forward.

When problems arise, our first reaction is to think of the worst scenario that could happen. We see only what is in front of us without realizing that there may be a simple solution to what we are going through. Our overthinking, mixed with fear, causes us to create an impossible scenario and a problem with no faith in resolution. Christians must look through God's eyes and see things as He sees them. By doing this, the problems become nothing but a triumph for God. He has our problems covered and promises us that we will never be alone. The key is not to give up under any circumstance! Nothing is impossible for God, and that includes our situation! Many of us jump to conclusions and mess up the entire scenario in the process. There is an ancient saying that "the devil takes a hand in what is done in haste," which is proven true more often than not—even today. The devil comes to us in various forms, especially when we are stuck in a situation that requires patience and hope.

At one time or another, each of us had given up when we were inches away from "reaping." Did you know that you were about to come out of the grave of problems if you just held on a little longer? We often fail to realize how close we are to success until we look in the rearview mirror because we would never give up if we knew how close we were. But this is where God wants us to blindly place our faith in Him and ask Him to deliver us. Nobody can truly understand and feel the pain the disciples faced daily when their messages were neglected or ridiculed in public. Yet they went on their way and continued to spread the good news and tell everyone about Jesus Christ through their actions. They knew they would get a far more valuable reward if they did this.

That is the time when your willpower is tested, and you need to ask yourself, "Am I done? Or do I have some gas left in the tank?" That question comes up often in your life, and you need to answer it very soon. You are the boss of your life. You are the boss of your capability. You are the boss of your mind. God has given you the power to choose. When you decide to get up after being knocked down, take time to care for yourself physically, spiritually, and emotionally and get back in the fight. It ends when you say it is over.

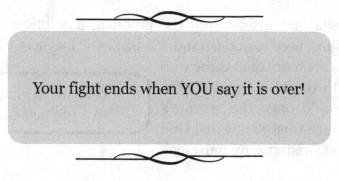

Your fight ends when YOU say it is over!

Your story is still being written.

As imperfect creations of God, we are bound to fail at some point. No one succeeds at every task they do—that is a truth that we must accept. We can use our failures as a lesson or allow them to be a stumbling block. The only way that failure can get the last word in our lives is if we choose to let it.

We serve a God who can take our defeats and missteps and still use us to bring glory to His name. Whether you have been walking with Him faithfully or you have had a few stumbles along the way, He is available to help you. Never give up.

God does not give up on us, so why are we giving up on ourselves? Do you remember Peter and how he walked on water? Most of us only think of how Peter lost focus on Jesus and then began to sink. However, the truth is Peter walked on water (see Matthew 6:22–36 NKJV)! As long as Peter stayed focused on Jesus and didn't look at the storm around him, he was OK. The same is true for you.

Second Kings 6:8–23 (NKJV) describes the story of Elisha and his servants. The Syrian army was camped around the city with many soldiers. The army had surrounded the city, and there was no way to escape. Elisha's servant came to him in great fear and anxiety, "What shall we do?" The servant could only see the problem through his eyes, which looked like it was impossible to overcome. Worry grabbed this servant of Elisha.

Elisha had insight into the problem, a solution we, as Christians, need to understand. Elisha knew "for those who are with us are more than those who are with them." He prayed that God would open the servant's eyes to see what Elisha and God saw. As Christians, we must look

> God deals in glory, not problems.

through God's eyes and see things as God sees them. By doing this, the problems become nothing but a triumph for God.

The servant's eyes were opened, and he could see_God's army surrounding the Syrian army on the hilltop. God has our problems covered, and He promises us that He will be with us "always, even to the end of the age" (Matthew 28:20 and Romans 8:31 NKJV). Philippians 4:13 (NKJV) says, "I can do all things through Christ who strengthens me."

Instead of merely looking for solutions, let's see how God can be glorified_through the promise He gave us.

So many things cry for our attention and devotion. Our jobs, children, spouses, and interests are the demands and distractions of life. Furthermore, we must be cautious not to let them become more of a priority than building a connection with the Holy Spirit. In doing so, we can see through God's eyes and never give up.

Nine or ten years ago, a man ministered to those living in a housing project, and he met a grandmother who lived there. He started studying and sharing God's Word with her. It was a slow process to get her close to obeying the gospel. For nine years, they studied and struggled. At times, it seemed she was going further away rather than drawing closer to the truth. How easy it could have been to give up and walk away. He could have thought he was wasting his energy and time on this lady when he could focus on a more receptive person. When do you call it quits? One, two, or eight years—when? To make a long story short, she was baptized nine and a half years after they first started studying. Would she have obeyed God's plea if he had quit after nine years?

Psalm 27:14 (NKJV) says, "Wait on the Lord; Be of good courage, And He shall strengthen your heart; Wait, I say, on the Lord!"

We must ask ourselves, "Whose timeline are we working on—ours or God's?" We must let God do His thing on His timetable, not on ours. When we allow God to work at His pace, we allow Him to grant us deliverance that we do not realize we need. It is a form of obedience, and in the scriptures, obedience is rewarded every time. This reward is carried forward to the next generation.

Naaman, the commander of the king's army of Aram, was diagnosed with leprosy, a disease that led victims to be cast out of the city. Although he was a nobleman in the eyes of his master, he still had leprosy. After receiving a message to go to Israel to be cured, Naaman stopped at Elisha's house. There, a messenger of Elisha told Naaman to go and wash in the Jordan, and he would be cleansed. However, he had to dip himself seven times.

When do you quit in Jordan—five or six times? When is enough enough? If Naaman had quit after five or six times, nothing would have happened. It was the next dip that counted. Naaman obeyed the message from Elisha, and he was healed. When is enough enough? When we've done what God said.

If we are ready to listen and obey the commands of the Lord through His Word in the Bible, we will also be free from our problems. We will witness the power of God. That is why you must never give up whenever there is any challenge in your life. Turn to God and allow Him to use you as a means to bring His glory to life.

Be concerned with the call. Be concerned with the gift that God has placed in you. He has called you; it will come to pass. Look to Jesus Christ. Don't worry about anything. Don't worry about your life. Don't worry. Don't give up. Don't worry about the church or the ministry God has given to you. Don't worry about your family. Don't worry about the job. Don't worry about anything. God has your back. Thank Him, worship Him, and dance for it.

11

Advantages of
No Worries

But seek first the kingdom of God and His righteousness,
and all these things shall be added to you.

—Matthew 6:33 (NKJV)

There will always be a time when worries will get the best
of us, no matter how positive we may be. There are times
in our lives when we continue to worry and forget that there is
a way out of difficult times, regardless of how many times we
are reminded. The fact that our minds are constantly worrying
about our problems just makes us fall deeper into them. And
that is when we must leave it to someone capable of doing the
impossible to give us wisdom and faith to overcome.

We are made in the image of God, and that is something
we need to keep in mind every single time we open our eyes.
Moreover, when we confront any difficult time, whether small or
large, we need to learn to put our faith in the Father. It is a priority
that we need to have. We, as His people, need to seek God first
over worldly things. I mean salvation, obedience, and sharing of

the good news with others. We worry because we don't do what God wants us to do, so how can we expect Him to do the same?

That is why we continue to worry. Acts 3 (NJKV) talks about the encounter between Peter and John with a lame man who needed to be carried to the temple's gate every day. This man was someone who had worried all his life, wondering if he would ever walk again. Peter said, "Silver or gold I do not have, but what I do have I give you. In the name of Jesus Christ of Nazareth, walk." The man's feet became strong enough for him to jump. He leaped and kept praising God for this miracle. The people who clearly remembered him to be lame were filled with amazement. The man's worry was now gone as he witnessed the glory of God.

The Story of the Asian King

I recall a story about an Asian king who was unaware of the problems of his people. After his father had passed away, he decided to leave the kingdom and go out where his people were. When he got out, he found that his people were living in a horrid state of poverty. Feeling sorry for them, the king called them inside his kingdom and told all of them to take one item. The instruction was, whatever you see that is good, take that one item. They were delighted to hear that and accepted his request.

As they were busy searching for what they wanted, an elderly lady came up to the king and asked, "King, are you sure that whatever I see I should take?"

The king replied, "Yes." She went on the search as well but then came back again and asked if he was really sure, and the king said, "Yes, you can take any one thing that you want."

She went around several times and asked the same question. The last time the lady came to the king, he was left speechless. The elderly lady returned empty-handed and said, "I see you, and I will take you as my son." She knew whatever the king had would be hers, so she wanted him.

God wants the same thing from us. If we focus entirely on Jesus Christ, then whatever He has will be ours. Once we have what God has, we will never need to worry about anything else. We worry because we lack the understanding of what the Word of God says concerning us. It takes the Spirit of God to give us enlightenment so our faith can be strengthened.

If we focus entirely on Jesus Christ—who died on the cross, shed His blood for us, and was resurrected from the grave on the third day—that same Holy Spirit that resurrected Him is the same spirit that will resurrect us to our purpose here on earth for His glory.

My younger sister, Grace Forlu, a gospel artist, wrote a song that inspired me. The lyrics say,

> You see a mountain before you, but there is no way to climb.
>
> You see a river beside you, but there is no way to cross.
>
> Moving on is difficult, but you got to trust.
>
> Be still and listen closely.
>
> You will hear a voice that says, "Don't be afraid. Keep holding on. Hold on. Don't be afraid to keep holding on. Move on."
>
> Life has a way of making you feel discouraged.

Be strong and hope in the name of the Lord.

The name of the Lord is a mighty, strong tower.

The righteous run to it, and they are saved.

Most of the time, people will come up to you and give pep talks by saying, "Difficult times don't last long" or "Get up and move on from this." We forget that to implement this advice, we still must rely on God. Our God is the one who gives us the necessary boost in the form of wisdom and hope. We are the ones who choose to believe what we see. When God continues to give us a way out of our problems, we tend to completely ignore He is helping us and instead blame Him for putting us in the problem. We sit and worry about what will happen next. That is when we need to remember that God wants us to overcome life's challenges. Jesus said, "These things I have spoken unto you that in me ye might have peace."

*God's Word gives hope. We are the ones
that choose to believe what we see.*

John 16:33 (KJV) says, "These things I have spoken unto you, that in me ye might have peace. In the world ye shall have tribulation: but be of good cheer; I have overcome the world." In other words, we *will* have problems, but we mustn't let the problems have us! The Twelve that Jesus inspired and trained went through the trouble, even after receiving the gift of the Holy Spirit. In reality, their lives got a lot tougher from there onward, but they were still at peace and content with the task they accepted. God loves us enough to take us out of any

situation, especially when everyone tells you that you will be stuck in it forever. If you have yet to witness God's presence, I believe you are ready to receive a miracle today! You can be in the worst place now, and nobody will know, but God is there to deliver you.

Psalm 91:11–12 (NKJV) says, "For He shall give His angels charge over you, To keep you in all your ways. In their hands, they shall bear you up, Lest you dash your foot against a stone."

> ## Declaration Prayer
>
> I prophesy to you that today you shall move that stone in your marriage, ministry, finances, and job. You shall not stumble, you shall not crumble, and you shall not grumble. Every demonic stone in your way is removed today in Jesus's name.
>
> I prophesy that angels shall carry your care from today forward. Angels shall carry your children, spouse, ministry, and business; everything that is dear to you is in the hands of the angels. That is why the Bible says, "They shall bear thee up."

The Holy Spirit, our great comforter and helper, accompanied by the angels from heaven, are sent to watch over us just as they watched over Jesus Christ until He made the ultimate sacrifice and ascension into heaven, now seated at the right hand of the Father.

Our problems are like a big stone, similar to what they put in front of the tomb to block the entrance in those times. It was so heavy and massive that, at that time, it took more than just one person to roll it a couple of feet. The stone represents all the problems and worries that we come across in our lives.

Sometimes it comes one at a time, and sometimes it comes all at once. It is a roadblock in your path to success. We all need angels to assist us in jumping over the stones of hindrances in our lives.

Worry is all we do when we have problems in life, but there are ways to overcome them. You need to remember the following three things:

You Are Valuable

We are a valuable creation of God, and He wants us all to remember that we do not need to worry about trivial matters over which He controls. We should avoid "What shall we eat?" or "What shall we drink?" or "What shall we wear?" You are a valuable child of God, and you must remember that all your life. When you are labeled as valuable, you will not be ignored. God will bail you out if you are caught in trouble, just as Jesus bailed out His disciples in Matthew 17:27.

Have Faith in God

You need to have faith in God. I know how hard it is to have faith or confidence in anything without seeing the evidence of its existence. Better yet, take the example of a woman who had a blood ailment, but she touched Jesus's garment to be healed, not knowing if just a touch would be enough to heal her (Luke 8:43–48 NKJV). In 2 Chronicles 32:7–8 (NKJV), Hezekiah encourages His people when King Sennacherib threatens them. He reminds them that there is a greater power with them.

We too are called to remember that God is the greater power. His powers can't be matched, so a hopeless situation is nothing in front of it.

Seek, Pray, and Study His Word

Seek the kingdom of God.

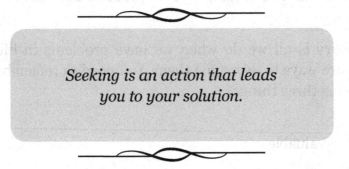

*Seeking is an action that leads
you to your solution.*

Be in the right standing with God, and everything will be added. Make God your number one priority. Spend time in the Word and live a life of fasting and praying.

Conclusion

Living a life without any worry improves our health in general. When we worry, we stress more and more, affecting our minds and causing health problems like heart disease and high blood pressure. A life of no worry can also improve our relationship with God and others. We tend to worry less about people's thoughts when prioritizing God in whatever we do.

Worry robs us of the quality of life we could experience. Trust God with the details of your life. He has the answers to the questions you're wrestling with. The more you turn those things over to Jesus, the more *peace* you'll have room to receive.

Consider this if you hear Jezebel speak from the throne of darkness. You'd think God's prophets will not last another day. She doesn't understand that they're God's properties, not man's properties! She doesn't know if the dogs will have her for lunch. Haman might have dug a pit to hang you but doesn't know that the pit he dug to harm you is for him, not you. Don't worry, God has your back.

Step out there and do something you've never done before. Reinvent yourself if you need to. Our capacity to receive the new is predicated on our ability to let go of old thinking patterns. We can sabotage our tomorrow if we're unwilling to embrace change. No change, no potential for growth. Change may just be the catalyst you need to keep flourishing. Get yourself involved in a Bible-believing church and stay committed. Associate yourself with the right people. Never lose your praise. Worship and superdance unto the Lord Jesus.

Holy Spirit Encounter of Grace Forlu, My Sister

Storm Versus Path

Some years back, during winter, it was announced that there'd be a heavy snowstorm. I was glad to hear that because that meant I wouldn't have to go to work. There was no such thing as "remote work" back then.

I asked my boss after several hours of the snow pouring if the office was still open, and she said yes. Needless to say, a girl was disgruntled, and her lazy agenda didn't happen (he-he-he, hi, Hanni).

As I murmured (like Miriam in the Bible) and sluggishly went upstairs to get ready for work, the Holy Spirit told me to go stand by the window and look over the balcony. Here's how that conversation went, and here's your lesson and encouragement:

Holy Spirit: Is it snowing, Grace?

Me: Yes.

Holy Spirit: Heavily?

Me: Well, yeah.

Holy Spirit: Are the roads being covered in snow?

Me: (Looking around at the street, I noticed the snow was melting and wasn't piling up) No.

Holy Spirit: Just because there's a storm doesn't mean the route to your destination isn't clear.

I was like 😲😔🐱.

Holy Spirit: Many people don't move or progress because they are waiting for the storm to pass, even if their route isn't affected.

Today, I come to encourage you to trust God through it all. Like the little boy's voice, say "I trust You, God. I trust You" while in the storm. Even in waiting, there's progress. Though I walk through the valley... don't stand, else, the waters will catch up with you.

God loves you deeply. Seek Him and obey Him, and it shall be well with you.

DANGEROUS PRAYER AGAINST THE SPIRIT OF WORRY

"God is to us a God of acts of salvation; and to God the LORD belong escapes from death [setting us free]" (Psalm 68:20 AMP).

1. Address the Father in Praise and Worship

Heavenly Father, holy is Your name and greatly to be praised. I worship and adore You in Jesus's name. May Your kingdom manifest in my life as it is in heaven. Plead my cause, O Lord, with those who strive with me; fight against any entity or person who is contending against me. Heavenly Father, it is written in Psalm 27:6 (AMP), "And now my head will be lifted up above my enemies around me, in His tent I will offer sacrifices with shouts of joy; I will sing, yes, I will sing praises to the Lord." Abba, I enjoin my worship to the heavenly chorus of worship of Your holy angels and the crowd of witnesses in Jesus's name.

2. Ask for the Court to Be Seated

Heavenly Father, Righteous Judge, I ask that the courts of heaven be seated according to Daniel 7:9–10 (AMP). I ask this in Jesus's mighty name. It is written: "I kept looking until thrones were set up, and the Ancient of Days [God] took His seat; His garment was white as snow and the hair of His head like pure wool. His throne was flames of fire; its wheels were a burning fire. A river of fire was flowing and coming out from

205

before Him; a thousand thousands were attending Him, and ten thousand times ten thousand were standing before Him; the court was seated, and the books were opened."

Heavenly Father, I am requesting the privilege of standing before the courtroom of the Ancient of Days, according to what was revealed to the prophet Daniel. In Jesus's name, I pray. Heavenly Father, I stand in Your royal courtroom because of the blood and finished work of Jesus on the cross. I have come to receive Your righteous judgment over my life against all familiar spirits and evil altars of worry, discouragement, intimidation, fear, and isolation that Satan planted in my generational bloodline. Heavenly Father, I call upon Your holy angels to be witnesses to my lawsuit and righteous prosecution of these evil altars and familiar spirits. I decree and declare that these evil altars of worry, discouragement, intimidation, fear, and isolation will not destroy me or my family. In Jesus's name, I pray.

3. Surrender Your Rights to Self-Representation to the Lord as Your Advocate

Heavenly Father, Your Word in 1 John 2:1–2 (NKJV) says, "My little children, these things I write to you, so that you may not sin. And if anyone sins, we have an Advocate with the Father, Jesus Christ the righteous. And He Himself is the propitiation for our sins, and not for ours only but also for the whole world." I thank You that Jesus is my faithful advocate before the Righteous Judge in the courts of heaven. Lord Jesus, I surrender my rights to self-representation and summon You as my advocate to help me plead my case before the Righteous Judge and prosecute the evil of altars of worry, discouragement, intimidation, fear, and isolation that Satan planted in my bloodline. I also ask the blessed Holy Spirit, who is the highest officer of the courts of heaven here on earth, to make me sensitive to the proceedings of this court to successfully prosecute these evil altars in Jesus's name.

4. Summon the Evil Altar and the Idol That Sits on It to Appear in Court

Heavenly Father, even as I stand in Your royal courtroom, I present myself as a living sacrifice, holy and acceptable before You according to Romans 12:1 (AMP). Heavenly Father, Righteous Judge, I summon the altars of worry, discouragement, intimidation, fear, and isolation in my bloodline and all the idols (demons) that operate on these altars to appear in Your royal courtroom to face prosecution in Jesus's name. For it is written in 1 Corinthians 6:3 (AMP), "Do you not know that we [believers] will judge angels? How much more then [as to] matters of this life?" Heavenly Father, I exercise my God-given authority in Christ Jesus to judge demons and principalities. In Jesus's name, I pray. Righteous Judge, it is also written in the constitution of Your kingdom in 1 John 3:8 (NKJV), "For this purpose the Son of God was manifested, that He might destroy the works of the devil."

5. Address Satan's Accusations and Agree with the Adversary

Heavenly Father, I know that until the end of the age of sin, Satan still has legal access to the courts of heaven to level accusations against the children of men, for it is written in the book of Revelation 12:10 (AMP):

> Then I heard a loud voice in heaven, saying, "Now the salvation, and the power, and the kingdom [dominion, reign] of our God, and the authority of His Christ have come; for the accuser of our [believing] brothers and sisters has been thrown down [at last], he who accuses them and keeps

bringing charges [of sinful behavior] against them before our God day and night."

Heavenly Father, the Lord Jesus also said in Matthew 5:25 (AMP):

Come to terms quickly [at the earliest opportunity] with your opponent at law while you are with him on the way [to court], so that your opponent does not hand you over to the judge, and the judge to the guard, and you are thrown into prison.

Heavenly Father, in all humility, while renouncing the spirit of pride, I choose to quickly agree with the legal accusations of my adversary, Satan. Righteous Judge, every accusation that Satan has filed against me and my bloodline in this court is true.

6. Repent

Heavenly Father, I repent for my personal transgressions and for the sins and iniquities of my forefathers that opened the door for the spirits and evil altars of worry, discouragement, intimidation, fear, and isolation to control my life. In Jesus's name, I pray. Lord, every sin of my forefathers that the enemy is using as a legal right to build cases against me and to marry me to worry, discouragement, intimidation, fear, and isolation, I ask that the blood of Jesus would just wash them away. I also repent for self-inflicted word curses and all covenants with demons that have existed in my ancestral bloodline. I am asking that every covenant with demonic powers will now be revoked and that their right to claim me and my bloodline would now be dismissed before Your court in Jesus's name. Thank You, Lord, for revoking these demonic covenants and evil altars in Jesus's mighty name! Heavenly Father, in my heartfelt desire to divorce myself from all familiar spirits and evil altars of worry, discouragement, intimidation, fear, and isolation, I give back everything and anything that the devil would say came from his kingdom. I only want what the blood of Jesus has secured for me.

7. Appeal to the Blood of Jesus to Wipe Out All Sin (Satan's Evidence)

Lord Jesus, thank You for cleansing me by Your blood so Satan has no legal footing against me in Your courtroom. It is written in 1 John 1:9 (AMP):

> If we [freely] admit that we have sinned and confess our sins, He is faithful and just [true to His own nature and promises] and will forgive our sins and cleanse us continually from all unrighteousness [our wrongdoing, everything not in conformity with His will and purpose].

Righteous Judge, I appeal to the blood of Jesus to wipe out all my shortcomings, transgressions, and iniquities. In Jesus's name, I pray. I receive by faith the cleansing power of the blood of Jesus.

8. Ask the Court to Dismiss All of Satan's Accusations and Charges

Heavenly Father, based upon Jesus's finished work and my heartfelt repentance, I now move to the court of heaven to dismiss all of Satan's accusations and charges against me and my bloodline in Jesus's name. For it is written in Revelation 12:10 (NKJV), "For the accuser of our brethren, who accused them before our God day and night, has been cast down." I ask you, Father, to cast down all of Satan's accusations against me. In Jesus's name, I pray.

9. Ask the Lord to Send Angels to Destroy the Evil Altar and Execute the Lord's Judgment Against It

Heavenly Father, Righteous Judge, I ask that You send high-ranking angelic officers of the courts who excel in strength to execute the judgment of Your supreme court and destroy the evil altars of worry, discouragement, intimidation, fear, and isolation and the idols that sit on them that Satan planted in my bloodline. In Jesus's name, I pray. By the spirit of prophecy, I prophesy the complete destruction of the evil altars of worry, discouragement, intimidation, fear, and isolation in my life in Jesus's name. For it is written in Psalm 91:11–12 (AMP), "For He will command His angels regarding you, to protect and defend and guard you in all your ways [of obedience and service]. They will lift you up in their hands, so that you do not [even] strike your foot against a stone." I receive angelic assistance right now in Jesus's name.

10. Present Scriptures That Will Be Used in Issuing a Divine Restraining Order

Heavenly Father, I present before Your supreme court the following scriptures as my rock-solid evidence against the spirits and altars of worry, discouragement, intimidation, fear, and isolation in my life. It is written:

> He shall call upon Me, and I will answer him; I will be with him in trouble; I will deliver him and honor him. With long life I will satisfy him and show him My salvation. (Psalm 91:15–16 NKJV)

> The thief does not come except to steal, and to kill, and to destroy. I have come that they may have life, and that they may have it more abundantly. (John 10:10 NKJV)

I shall not die but live and declare the works and recount the illustrious acts of the Lord. (Psalm 118:17 AMPC)

Righteous Judge, based upon the aforementioned scriptures, it is clear that the spirits and evil altars of worry, discouragement, intimidation, fear, and isolation, if allowed to succeed, would cause great injury to my life and destiny and also inflict irreparable damage to the purposes of God. I ask that every legal right these spirits and altars of worry, discouragement, intimidation, fear, and isolation are holding be revoked in Jesus's glorious name. Righteous Judge, based upon the aforementioned scriptures, it is clear that I qualify for a divine restraining order against these evil altars of worry, discouragement, intimidation, fear, and isolation and the familiar spirits that sit on them in Jesus's name.

11. Ask the Court to Issue a Divine Restraining Order and Receive the Divine Restraining Order by Faith

Heavenly Father, Righteous Judge, I now ask that a divine restraining order and a permanent injunction against the spirits and altars of worry, discouragement, intimidation, fear, and isolation in my life would now be issued by the authority of Your supreme court in Jesus's name. Heavenly Father, I decree and declare that all plans the devil has issued or is orchestrating against my life are now canceled in Jesus's glorious name. Heavenly Father, I receive this divine restraining order and permanent injunction by faith in Jesus's name. For it is written in the constitution of Your kingdom in Hebrews 11:6 (AMP), "But without faith it is impossible to [walk with God and] please Him, for whoever comes [near] to God must [necessarily] believe that God exists and that He rewards those who [earnestly and diligently] seek Him." I believe and declare by faith that the spirits and altars of worry, discouragement, intimidation, fear, and isolation in my life have been judged in Jesus's name!

12. Ask the Lord to Seal Your Righteous Verdict and Court Proceedings in the Blood of Jesus

Heavenly Father, Righteous Judge, I now ask You to seal my righteous verdict against the spirits and altars of worry, discouragement, intimidation, fear, and isolation in the precious blood of Jesus. May You also cover with the blood of Jesus all my legal proceedings in this court in Jesus's name. I decree and declare that my righteous verdict of release and breakthrough from the evil altars of worry, discouragement, intimidation, fear, and isolation is now secured in the documents of the courts of heaven. For it is written in John 8:36 (AMP), "So if the Son makes you free, then you are unquestionably free." I decree and declare that I am free of the evil altars of worry, discouragement, intimidation, fear, and isolation, in Jesus's name. Amen!

Don't worry, God has your back.

Printed in the United States
by Baker & Taylor Publisher Services